Discover Your BUSINESS POWER

NIKKOS ZORBAS

Insights for Genuine Self Leadership

Discover Your Business Power by Nikkos Zorbas
Copyright © 2014 by Nikkos Zorbas
Published in the U.S.A. by Positive Impact Press

POSITIVE IMPACT PRESS

Cover design by Rhett Nielson
Interior design by Ren Cummins
ISBN-10: 1499368712
ISBN-13:978-1499368710

ALSO BY NIKKOS ZORBAS:

Discovering your Personal Power
The Reveal: Build a Big Dream Journal

AUDIO PROGRAMS:
The Reveal: Dream Big, Never Quit
The Law of Attraction Music Album

Table of Contents

INTRODUCTION

When it comes to success in business, the most important thing to remember is that each step along the way is driven by your thoughts and ideas. Your life experience, both personal and professional, is a collection of every thought you've ever had. Everything ever created began with a thought, which then developed into a vision. Before I wrote this book, I envisioned it. Helen Keller said, "The only thing worse than being blind is having sight but no vision."

Unfortunately, many of us go through our daily routines in a trance-like state. When this occurs we give up our power of conscious choice, and as a result all decision making is made by default. If we don't control our choices, other people and society in general will do it for us. And that is where the real danger comes in.

So it's up to you to take control and organize your thoughts and ideas, and in a way that they enable you to start and continue on a path to a fulfilled life. But what is the best way to take control? I believe the ancient Greek philosopher Socrates said it best in two very simple words: "Know thyself."

That's right. The answers to all you will ever need to reach your goals are already within you. It is only when you lose touch with your inner true self that you begin to stray and become confused about your purpose and direction in life. And how can you effectively lead others if you're ineffective in leading yourself?

By reading this book, you are consciously choosing to learn tips and techniques on how to identify and work toward your goals and be a genuine leader from the inside out. I suggest you read it again and again, and take notes on the areas that pertain to your current situation. You'll see that some tips from some of the insights may coincide with others. This was intentional since different areas of life overlap as well. It's a good idea to keep the book handy and refer to certain chapters as you need them.

Congratulate yourself for taking this first step. Let the journey begin!

Discover Your
BUSINESS
POWER

Insight 1:

Claim Your Personal Power

"True happiness involves the full use of one's power and talents."

~John W. Gardner

U sually when I ask people what they want out of life, their answer involves something they don't have. I then ask, "Why don't you have it yet?" They typically respond with a lame and over-rationalized excuse that may sound good to them, but they're not fooling me!

The fact is, if you are not living the life you always desired to have, you are subconsciously rebelling against yourself. By that I mean you have no faith in your personal power, or you refuse to exercise it. Personal power is the foundation of your power in business. It encompasses strength, confidence, and competence, and the lack of personal power makes it almost impossible to achieve your business goals.

Fortunately, personal power can be cultivated. Here are some easy ways to claim your personal power and get on the path to enjoying the life you were meant to live.

9

- **Set worthy goals and construct your life around them.** Remember, your goals and the effort you put into them determine the outcome of your life.

- **Once you begin a project, make sure you follow it through to completion.** You may reach a satisfying completion, meaning you've achieved what you set out to do, or sometimes you reach an impasse that allows you to go no further. Either way, a project is considered completed once you've gone as far as you can go with it. It's better to abandon a project than have it hang over your head.

- **Make sure your actions match your words.** If they don't, you diminish your credibility and, therefore, your power.

- **Learn to embrace problems; they stimulate your analytic mind.** Remember, if there were no problems, most of us would not have a job or own a business. (Tip: If you want a higher salary, change the size of the problems you solve.)

- **Always under-promise and over-deliver.** When you deliver more than what's expected, it's almost impossible to fail. This applies to both your professional and personal lives. Employees who practice this become a hot commodity; employers will do whatever it takes to keep them, including raising their salaries. Business owners who over-deliver will enjoy loyal customers who will tell others about the exceptional value they received.

- **Practice excellence in all that you do.** Anything that's worth doing is worth doing well. Besides, this helps attract all the right people and circumstances into your life.

- **Stay clear of stressful people and avoid stressful situations.** The only ones who benefit from stress are the media, politicians, doctors and drug companies. Why add to their profits when you should be adding to your own?

- **Speak well and considerately.** Never finish another person's sentence or speak over them. Use proper grammar, develop your vocabulary, and choose your words wisely. Every time you speak you are either moving closer to or further away from your goals. This applies not only to your external dialogue, but to your internal dialogue as well, meaning the things you say to yourself.

- **Be a people person**. Value your connections with others and increase your networking activities. Networking is more than simply handing out your business card; think of it as relationship building. I can't begin to tell you how many business cards I've collected over the years that ended up in the trash because there was no relationship behind them.

- **Do a mental inventory or keep a list of all the people you know well and their specific skills.** That way you'll know whom to call on for advice or help.

- **Understand where your weaknesses lie, and make an effort to strengthen them.** Give them the attention they need in order to conquer them.

- **If you make a mistake, own it and move forward fast.** Learn from what went wrong, but don't dwell on your misstep or beat yourself up. Instead, focus your energy on new solutions.

- **Protect your reputation.** If anyone tries to tarnish it, fight back with professionalism and tact. This world is full of people who would like nothing more than to see you fail. Don't allow their opinions to become your truth.

The bottom line is, if you are not doing all you are capable of doing to become all that you are capable of becoming, it's your own fault. By claiming your personal power, you're on the way to claiming all the good things in life you deserve – including your professional dreams!

Insight 2:

Succeed In Good Times or Bad

"Bad times have a scientific value. These are occasions a good learner would not miss."

~Ralph Waldo Emerson

No doubt about it; countries experience recessions from time to time. As a result, people become stressed out, depressed and confused, it's no wonder the use of anti-depression medication in the United States has doubled in recent years. And the effect is global; anti-depressant use all around the world had been rapidly increasing.

While there may not be much you can do about the state of the world economy, there is a lot you can do about your personal economic and emotional state. Just remember one thing: this country has been hit by a recession before and during those times, many people were able to prosper.

That's right. Many people lost everything and rebuilt from nothing to become some of the wealthiest individuals in the world. For example, a man named Charles Darrow found himself unemployed after the 1929 market crash. He then invested his time perfecting a home-made board game in which the object was to buy and sell property. That game is now known as Monopoly, and Darrow became the world's first millionaire game designer.

Regardless of economic conditions, opportunity is all around us. Both businesses and individuals will always have needs to fill. During the Great Depression the movie industry exploded because people needed an emotional release. Movies created a temporary escape from the stress and worry many were experiencing, and despite how tight money was at the time, people were still willing to pay the price of a movie ticket.

My friend Jen Ashton, who also wrote the forward in my book, *Discovering Your Personal Power*, told me about when she was at the lowest point in her life. She lost not only her home, but her car and all her important possessions in her storage unit, too. Jen was flat broke and to top it off, her boyfriend left her. Lost, confused and with her seven-year-old son to care for, Jen dug deep inside her gut and found a need to fulfill. Capitalizing on her background in creative marketing and business consulting, she became a bestselling Kindle author, and within a year's time, she became a shareholder of a successful restaurant chain. Recently she purchased the car of her dreams. Jen has become financially independent, and is living happily.

These stories are just the tip of the iceberg. There are thousands of similar tales of success, and they serve as proof that if someone else can do it, so can you!

One of the key formulas for becoming successful during a recession is the ability to recognize opportunity and stay the course. Don't become a life-long soul searcher or procrastinator. It's time to get serious about where you want to be and create a road map to take you there. Plan and prepare instead of sleep and dream! Dreams don't matter unless you're awake and making them happen.

I hear the same story over and over again and often from some people: "Now I am going to make things happen... This is the year for me!" The reason this happens is people operate on autopilot and aren't truly conscious of their decisions and what they are doing. And so they repeat the cycle over and over again.

Here are some questions to consider as you plan for your dreams :

1. What did I promise I was going to accomplish before?

2. What did I accomplish?

3. What would I do differently?

The key is to wake up your awareness level and make a conscious effort to attain the life you really want. For some people, like Charles Darrow and my friend Jen, it takes a serious life event for this to happen. Why wait for that to happen to you? Be proactive, not reactive!

So, remember to recognize and identify opportunity, know that others have proven it can be done, and keep yourself in check. Jen Ashton changed her world. The late Steve Jobs, founder of Apple computers, proved how one man can change the world...what can you do? Most importantly, what *will* you do? Make it happen!

Insight 2: Succeed In Good Times or Bad

Insight 3:

Act Like a True Professional

"Professionalism is knowing how to do it, when to do it, and doing it!"

~Frank Tyger

E veryone seems quick to lament, "It's the economy!" But when one is struggling to be successful, is the economy really to blame? I know business people who are extremely successful in this economy and some who are not. The ones who aren't seem to blame the economy. I believe they should be blaming themselves.

Why? What are they doing wrong? Many of them need to cultivate a greater sense of professionalism. Unprofessional practices are being seen today in epidemic proportions! So many people call themselves professionals, yet for many, their behavior betrays their self image.

I personally have witnessed individuals in many fields—including real estate, photography, law, food service, medical, and physical fitness to name a few—refer to themselves as professionals. I wonder how well I'm able to hide the stunned look on my face. *"How can that be?"* I wonder. How can these people expect to make a living—much less call

17

themselves "professional"—when they provide such horrific service?

The principles for true professionalism do not require years of study and complicated graphs. No, true professionalism is derived from a common sense approach that anyone can understand and apply. A sense of professionalism isn't just for business owners—whether you're an entrepreneur, employee, or just looking to get ahead in life, follow these principles and be prepared to meet success.

- **Know your strong points!** It's important that others perceive you as competent in what you do. To call yourself an expert, you must stay on the leading edge of your discipline. Commit yourself to life-long learning and never pass up an opportunity to educate yourself.

- **Speak with confidence.** Be a fluid communicator; eliminate the "ums" and "uhs" from your vocabulary. When you have a solid understand of your field, this should be easy to do. Strong communication skills add to your credibility, and people will feel confident doing business with you.

- **Develop a disciplined approach to your work.** If you find it difficult to focus, you're probably lacking in passion. That means you could be in the wrong vocation, or need to rediscover the joy in your work and why you were drawn to it in the first place. You then keep that passion alive my making sure your goals remain on the forefront of your mind. People will sense your passion and will want to do business with you. Remember, discipline equals results, and passion equals energy!

- **Do not be tempted by greed.** This means you must place your clients' best interests first and focus on their needs, not how much money you will make from them. If you're in a commission-based job, do not try to sell your client on what will give you the most commission. Instead, offer what's the best solution to meet their needs. You will end up ahead in the long run because you will build the best sales tool in the world: a strong and honest reputation. Do this and money will follow. Remember, the client is number one!

- **Don't take your customers' money if they are unhappy with your work, product or services.** Make it right before you accept payment!

- **Show that you're interested in your customers beyond just what they can do for you.** When you are with a client, give your entire attention to that person. Make sure your clients feel they're your whole world at that moment. Remember that although winning the business of first-time customers is a nice accomplishment, a true professional knows how to keep them coming back. The fake professionals may boast when they get a sale and tell themselves and others how great they are; however, they are only fooling themselves. Their success will be short-lived and is sure to be followed by struggle.

- **Set realistic expectations**. You can have the best product or service in the world, but if you fail to deliver when you say you will, all that value is diminished. You can't go wrong with the old saying, "Under-promise and over-deliver!"

- **Always ask yourself, "How can I serve my customers better?"** Ask for their input on how you can be of better service to them—they'll appreciate that!

In order to thrive in any economy, you must master the skills of what it takes to be a true professional. True professionalism is not just about having expertise in a given field; it's about believing wholeheartedly in what you do. It's about going all out for your clients, by making their best

19

interest a priority. It's about never compromising your values or lowering your standards.

When you act with true professionalism, you take control of your own personal economy and write your own ticket to success!

Insight 4:

Stop Procrastinating and Jumpstart Your Life

"Procrastination is one of the most common and deadliest of diseases and its toll on success and happiness is heavy".

~Wayne Gretzky

A re you tired of not having the life you've always dreamed of? What if you could change everything by eliminating one word from the way you live today?

That word is procrastination. Too many people are master procrastinators, putting off their dreams for another day. Some have given up completely and will spend most of their lives complaining about how unlucky they are. They will remain blind to the opportunities they are presented with, rather than act upon them.

Procrastination is a dream stealer, and its effects can be costly. For example, many people pay for a gym membership, yet procrastinate and hardly ever use it. Instead of wasting their money, they would be better off giving it to a worthy cause.

So what is procrastination? Simply put, procrastination is the act of giving in to negative habits. These become new

21

habits and slowly form a lifestyle. Procrastination can be overcome by weakening the negative habits and consciously cultivating positive habits to replace this pattern. This is why top professional athletes tell you their secret is, "Practice, practice, practice." By training your mind, you're making the greatest investment in your future.

Since you have already put many hours into activities to live your current lifestyle, why not invest several minutes each day into creating your ultimate existence? Here are some steps to master in order to avoid procrastination and jumpstart your life:

- **Define what success means to you.** Visualize, in detail, where you want to be.
- **Identify the activities that must be done to get to where you want to be**. In other words, make your goals seem simpler and more doable by breaking them down into smaller tasks. Consider each step to be a goal in itself. For example, let's say you want to get fit. Maybe you could set a goal to run one mile every other day. Begin by walking once around the block for a week, then the following week jog around the block, and build from there.
- **Write down each goal**. Sadly, only three people out of a hundred bother to do this. Once your goals are on paper, read them out loud. Hearing yourself articulate your goals in your own voice makes them more real.
- **Set a timeframe to accomplish each goal**. Purchase a day planner or use a smart phone app to keep yourself on track.
- **Quit making excuses**. You may have heard someone--maybe even yourself--say, "If only I were younger..." Well, Thomas Edison still worked on inventions even after he was 90 years old, and Michelangelo did some of his best work after the age of 80. You are never too

old, or too young, to set worthwhile goals. Other excuses include "I don't have time" and "I have no money." Find a way to make the time, and remember, billionaire Howard Schultz, founder of Starbucks, grew up in a housing project in Brooklyn, New York. No excuses!

- **Identify the people who give you energy**. Share your goals with them. By letting them know of your intentions, you also become accountable for your actions.
- **Avoid people who instill doubt**. Anyone who is less than supportive will only drag you down.
- **Think of the consequences of delaying action**. What would your life look like if you don't begin to work on your goals now?
- **Surround yourself with things that inspire victory**. Not just photos or mementos of your past accomplishments; include some that inspire your future, of where you are going and want to be.
- **Create two separate bucket lists, one for the short-term and the other for decades to come**. Make sure to integrate these items into your daily planning.
- **Organize your environment**. This will help organize your thoughts. De-clutter and live by the adage, "A place for everything, and everything in its place!" It's that simple.
- **At the end of the day, take 15 minutes to organize your thoughts and prepare for tomorrow**. It will be much easier to get things done when you know exactly what they are.

The bottom line is, don't let the negative habit of procrastination hold you back any longer. Procrastination is like skydiving with a parachute half open; you might still make it to the ground, but with a lot more anxiety and most likely you will not land on your intended target.

Insight 4: Stop Procrastinating and Jump Start Your Life

Insight 5:

Get Back on Track with Inspiration from Others

"Good actions give strength to ourselves and inspire good actions in others."

~Plato

We all go through times when everything and everyone seems to be against us and nothing is going right. You may question every decision you've ever made, wondering what your life would look like if you'd taken another path. Most of the time, this feeling of malaise is fleeting and all that's needed to dig yourself out of that hole is a change of perspective.

While you're experiencing a blue period, it's helpful to keep in mind that individuals before you have also endured tremendous struggles and adversity, and have gone on to become some of the most successful people in this world. Athletes, entertainers, and everyday people like us have emerged from periods of doubt and adversity, sometimes overcoming incredible odds. Almost everyone—including folks in your own social circle—has a story you can learn from and apply to your own life.

As for me, I've been personally inspired by my friend, Rudy Ruettiger, the man behind the 1993 blockbuster movie *Rudy*. Rudy and I met a few years back over dinner. I had just finished recording my inspirational music album, *The Law of Attraction* and Rudy happened to be back in town from a speaking tour.

The movie *Rudy* is based on his life story, specifically his determination to fulfill his dream of playing football for Notre Dame despite the incredible odds against him. Rudy came from a family without much money, was small in stature, and everyone told him he wouldn't make it. Because he suffered from dyslexia at a time before such a condition was properly recognized, he was never considered to be very smart. In fact, one of his school teachers even told him he was stupid. But as a result of his undying spirit, he managed to graduate from the University of Notre Dame and played in the final home game of the season.

Playing football for Notre Dame would not be Rudy's only life challenge. He has another story not too many people know about, the story of what it took for him to get the film made.

You see, not only had Rudy never written a film script before, he knew absolutely nothing about what it would take to make a movie and had no connections in the business. But what he did have was a lot of vision, patience and tenacity. He didn't listen to the naysayers; he listened only to the few people who told him he could do it. He learned to ignore what Rudy calls "goofy thoughts," the thoughts that tell you, "It's not worth it" or "It can't be done." Had Rudy allowed those goofy thoughts to take over his mind, the fifty-fourth most inspiring film of all time by the American Film Institute would not be called *Rudy*.

We all have dreams buried inside of us. The problem is, most of us don't believe in them. Many people take the word "believe" for granted, yet it's probably the most powerful word ever written since everything in your life is about belief. You eat because you believe if you don't, you will die. You believe that if you jump off a tall building, you would most likely be killed.

The key to manifesting your desires boils down to two words: eliminating doubt. Doubt is the number one killer of dreams. We are all familiar with doubt, but doubt can be eliminated by believing. Belief kills doubt. And the most important thing to believe in when you want to manifest your dreams is yourself. Beliefs are so powerful, that whatever you believe—whether it's true or not—you're right! "Behave, believe, and become," Rudy always says. This will attract good energy toward yourself and will fuel your dreams.

Belief is the most powerful force in the world, and when you learn to utilize it to your advantage you become unstoppable. You must clear out any beliefs that are not serving you. Always ask yourself, "Is what I currently believe bringing me closer or further from my goals?"

Everyone experiences low periods of life, filled with self-doubt. What do these periods teach us? That life is a process, a series of ebbs and flows. Sometimes we fall off our path to success or become overwhelmed by the obstacles we face. Circumstances such as extreme financial issues, emotional or physical scars, or suffering as a result of traumatic loss can cause us to lose our enthusiasm and greatly diminish our quality of life.

The question is, "How do I get back on my feet after I've been knocked down?" Just know there is a path for you, and your job is to get back on it and keep moving forward. Get back on the path of your true life's purpose and persevere. For inspiration, examine the lives of others who've been there, done that. If they can do it, so can you!

Insight 5: Get Back on Track with Inspiration from Others

Insight 6:

Embrace Your Problems

"Problems are not stop signs, they are guidelines."

~Robert Schuller

P roblems…we all have them. Simply put, problems represent the difference between how things are and how you want them to be.

No matter how hard we try to prevent them, problems in life are unavoidable. Since we will continue to have problems to some degree for the rest of our lives, why not take these steps to embrace, rather than resist, them?

- **Define the problem.** The first step is to understand exactly what the problem entails. This is important because you must learn to analyze a problem in order to find its proper solution. Look at the problem objectively and then break it down into smaller sections. Analyze each section from all sides; really study them. Sometimes you may be too close to a problem, so you must take a step back, sleep on it, and then see how it looks the next day. You may find that the problem is not even *your* problem; it's a situation that someone else needs to attend to. There's also the possibility that the problem is not worth solving. Never spend your time on petty problems that don't matter.

Instead, focus your life energy on the problems that have lasting values and rewards.

- **Gauge your reaction**. When faced with the same problem, two people can have two entirely different reactions to it. One can be stressed out and feeling victimized, while the other is challenged by the opportunity to make the situation better. The only difference between the two is how they perceive the problem.

- **Accept the situation and don't resist what is.** What you resist will persist. By approaching the problem with a positive attitude, you're already weakening its potency. The real problem comes when you begin to doubt your capabilities. Erase all self-defeating negative words from your vocabulary such as "won't," "can't," and "impossible." As human beings, we are born experts in problem solving; you're alive today because of your amazing ability to solve problems.

- **Visualize yourself already solving your problem**. Formulate a mental picture and hold it; your mind will seek to develop it. Eat, sleep and work as though you have beaten your problem.

- **Identify and implement a solution**. At this point, you've analyzed and accepted the situation. You're no longer focusing on the problem; your attention and energies are directed to the solution. Keep an open, creative mindset and know that the only way you can get to the next level is through tapping your limitless potential and intellectual power.

- **Find others who have solved similar problems**. Think of how one of your mentors would address this problem. Libraries are filled with thousands of books about people who have overcome major problems on their journeys to success. Educate yourself as much as possible on whatever it takes to solve the issue. Think of all the possibilities, choose the best ones and apply them.

- **Appreciate the opportunities a problem presents**. I know it's a bit cliché, but many problems truly are blessings in disguise.

A friend of mine telephoned me one afternoon in total despair. He had been fired after working for ten years at a popular upscale hotel. "Can I work for you?" he wanted to know.

"Why you would want to work for me when you can start that business you've always talked about?" I asked. "It seems that now is the time!" And so I helped him launch his new endeavor, which he built into a successful company. He now had true job security, and was proud that he could support his family through his own initiative.

My friend created a much more stable source of income, and it never would have happened had he not been faced with a problem. A problem opens doors to our future; it is the key for opportunity. I think everyone should write this on their mirrors and recite it every day:

"PROBLEMS ATTRACT OPPORTUNITY"

- **Be ready for next time.** With each problem we successfully address, we strengthen our problem solving muscles. For example, let's say you're facing a problem related to real estate transactions. If I were to ask, "Who do you think has bigger real estate problems, you or Donald Trump?" my guess is you would answer, "Donald Trump, of course!" If you were to give Donald Trump your real estate problems, he would consider them to be very small, and he would find a solution quickly. Donald Trump is extremely successful because he has developed big problem-solving muscles.

The degree of your success, in business and life in general, revolves around your problem solving skills. Make problem solving with a positive mental attitude a habit; become a master of the art of problem solving. You can't always choose your problems, but you can always choose your perception of them and learn to sharpen your ability to address them.

Insight 7:

Act Well When No One is Looking

"Character is what a man is in the dark."

~ Dwight L. Moody

P eople skills require the ability to communicate effectively with individuals of all types. However, what matters most is your true character, which is revealed by how you act when you think nobody is looking.

Everywhere you go and everything you do involves interactions with other individuals, sometimes on a personal level, sometimes while conducting business. The way you interact with others can have a dramatic impact on your life, and not always when you're aware of it.

For example, let's say Bob considers himself to be a savvy and successful salesman. He's about to close the biggest deal of his life with an important prospective client and he's working the Mr. Nice Guy persona in a major way. Later that day, Bob sees an elderly lady fall down in the street, but instead of offering his assistance, he just keeps walking. What Bob failed to realize is that his big client happened to be on the same street witnessing the entire event. The next day, to Bob's surprise, the client calls to say he has no interest in continuing their negotiations. Of course, Bob's failure to assist the elderly lady revealed to the potential client Bob's TRUE character.

Here's another example. In Sir Richard Branson's reality show *The Rebel Billionaire*, sixteen contestants competed for one of the most lucrative prizes in reality TV history. As it turned out, the competitors had completed their very first task without ever knowing it. Upon their arrival at the airport, Mr. Branson himself picked up the contestants disguised as a cab driver. Two of them addressed him in a rather cocky and demeaning manner. When Mr. Branson revealed his true identity, they were quickly fired.

The lesson from these two stories is that you should always treat people well, regardless of what you think they may or may not be able to do for you in return. You never know who they might turn out to be. That stranger you treat poorly might be the one person who could give you CPR in an emergency. Think of how you would treat that individual if you knew he would later save your life.

Here are some essential tips for developing people skills, whether or not anyone's around to notice:

- **Make an effort to understand others.** Learning to understand people in different situations is key. Let's say you're at a restaurant. The waitress seems a bit upset; you know she hasn't had a good day. Remember, people may act in a negative way to you, but how you respond to them is your choice. Instead of reacting with equal negativity and adding to her pain, do something to help alleviate it. Offer a sincere compliment or find something nice to say. You can make someone's day just by being pleasant, and you'll enjoy better customer service. Everybody benefits.
- **Be willing to learn from others**. If all your work is based solely on what you already know, you will eventually be overtaken by someone younger, smarter, or hungrier. Never stop learning and always be willing

to learn from others. The day you become unteachable will be the day you stop progressing in any endeavor. Treat others as the experts--this will earn you respect and admiration, as well as heighten their desire to work with you.

- **Listen more, talk less and ask questions**. How you listen to others is another important skill. Listening to someone with your full attention and allowing them to finish a sentence without your interrupting shows you are engaged in and value what they have to say. There's a reason we have two ears and one mouth!

- **Communicate clearly and to the point.** Don't beat around the bush. People respect and appreciate direct communication. It saves time and the effort of trying to piece together what you're getting at.

- **Remember that the least important word in a conversation is "I."** Enough about you; start talking in terms of "we."

- **Check your ego**. As some people gain success, their ego grows proportionately. There is what I call a healthy ego, but there is also an unhealthy ego. A healthy ego reflects the ability to deal with your emotions effectively and reacts in a positive way when faced with challenges. This is where true self-esteem reigns. An unhealthy ego involves boasting and putting others down, and basically tries to make up for one's insecurities and underlying low self-esteem. Whereas a healthy ego celebrates and contributes to the success of others, an unhealthy ego is consumed with jealousy and insecurity.

- **Refrain from judging and never put others down.** People make mistakes; nobody is perfect. When others display their imperfections, seize the opportunity to let your grace and charisma show them a better way.

- **Keep your word.** Always do what you say and make good on your promises. Having strong values and ethics is a sure way to build a great reputation. There's nothing better than having people refer to you as a "professional."

The bottom line: Always be respectful of others, even if you think they have nothing to offer you. You may not like the behavior they display, but that doesn't mean you can't like the individual. By combining these skills with a sincere attitude, you dramatically increase your chances for producing the best possible, win-win outcome.

Insight 8:

Understand the Power of Persuasion

"Character may almost be called the most effective means of persuasion."

~Aristotle

Whatever you want to do--whether it's ask for a raise, run for public office, or start your own business--your ability to persuade others will make the difference between success and failure.

I remember when I was 18 years old. I was in love and had a beautiful girlfriend, but unfortunately I had no job. I knew that a job with a nice title would surely impress her, as well as her parents, so I applied for a position as an electronic technician. Mind you, I had no idea what the job entailed or the specialized education it required, but I did like the professional sounding title.

The interviewer reviewed my application and, predictably, said she was sorry but she couldn't help me. However, I wanted that job and made up my mind not to leave her office without it. The interviewer could feel my sincerity and passion - I told her what this job would mean to me, what an asset I would be for the company, and that I could start right that

37

moment. She looked straight into my eyes and said, "I don't normally do this, but I am going to hire you. We will train you."

The bottom line is, through the power of persuasion, I was able to not only get a job for which I had absolutely no qualifications, but got free on-the-job training as well. Through the power of persuasion, I accomplished what most would deem impossible. From that experience, I learned that the world seems to support those who know what they want and have the innate ability to persuade others.

Persuasion is defined as the intent to influence another person's opinion, attitude or beliefs through the use of sounds, words and images. These may be physical, verbal, or nonverbal, and may be transmitted through media outlets such as radio and television, the Internet, billboards, and face-to-face communication.

For some people, the word *persuasion* has a negative connotation. This is because they are confusing persuasion with manipulation. Persuasion can be rewarding for all parties involved when applied in a positive manner with good intentions.

To understand the true power of persuasion, think about how many times you are persuaded every day, often without even realizing it. Whether you pull into a particular gas station, have a craving for a certain food item you saw in a TV commercial, or speak to a salesperson at a department store, you were attracted to these places and people by the power of persuasion.

Mastering effective persuasion will be one of the most life-changing resources in your arsenal of life skills. You can have the greatest talent, idea or product in the world, but if you lack the power of persuasion, you will probably go unnoticed.

To prevent this from happening to you, here are some specific techniques you can use to improve your power of persuasion:

- **When addressing others, know what you're talking about**. Present yourself as an expert. Speak clearly and be specific. Specificity builds credibility, which increases trust. Trust is the #1 key to effective persuasion.

- **Make sure the physical environment supports your goal**. This is important because a person's surroundings dictate his or her behavior. For instance, when you go to a movie, the smell of popcorn entices you to visit the concession stand. Similarly, make sure the environment you're in is conducive to ensuring the outcome you desire. For example, you shouldn't attempt to discuss sensitive topics in a bustling restaurant.

- **When presenting, selling, or teaching, allow time for and encourage people to take notes**. The act of writing down things you say helps to solidify their commitment; in a sense, they have invested in you. This increases rapport and the chance they will side with you or do business with you.

- **Take a keen—and sincere—interest in your audience, personally as well as professionally**. Provide solutions to their problems, and explain them as simply as possible. Demonstrate that you believe in them. At the end of your time together, show your gratification for the time they've spent with you.

- **Be likable!** Make sure you communicate with a pleasing and sincere personality. Deliver your message with enthusiasm. Remember, enthusiasm is contagious!

- **Develop the reputation as the person that gets things done**. Project the assumption that together you can conquer the world.

- **Be inspiring**. Even if you feel your audience has nothing to offer you, let them know that they, too, have the potential to become great.

Success isn't about making the correct decisions every single time--no person can do that. Yet persuasion (when used properly) will produce a positive outcome for all parties involved. An effective communicator knows how to utilize the power of persuasion so everyone wins!

Insight 9:

Overcome "Scattered Thinking Syndrome"

"A distracted existence leads us to no goal."

~Johann Wolfgang von Goethe

H ave you ever noticed how some people seem to accomplish a lot with minimal effort while others work hard, but have little to show for themselves? Chances are those individuals suffer from what I call "Scattered Thinking Syndrome."

What is STS? Here are some defining characteristics:

- People with STS are typically idea junkies who speak passionately about their grand plans for success, perhaps jumping from one get-rich-quick scheme to another. In conversation they are rarely good listeners, and seem oblivious to the fact that someone else might have something interesting to say.

- People with STS never seem to bring their ideas to fruition. It is hard for them to make a decision and even harder to follow up with action. That's because their thoughts are so unorganized and overwhelming that they become paralyzed, unable to make a move.

- People with STS are easily distracted and lack the ability to focus.

Does any of this sound like you? If so, the good news is, now you've realized it and can take action. Here are some tips to redirect your thinking for overcoming Scattered Thinking Syndrome:

- **Identify what you want to do**. This requires you to organize your thoughts. You will never know the true value and potential of your ideas, talents or training unless you organize your thoughts. Learn how to organize your thoughts effectively so that they serve you in a positive and fulfilling way.

- **Make sure the task is worth doing**. Is it in line with your overall goals? Make sure you say "yes" to the things that really matter in your life and "no" to the things that don't. There's no point in expending energy on something that doesn't matter. Think of the value the achievement of each goal will bring to your life, and keep that feeling on the forefront of your mind. The ability to recognize the value of achieving certain goals in your life is key to your success.

- **Give the task your undivided attention**. Let's say you need to send out an important email. While you're writing, do you check to see what your friends are doing on Facebook? Are you simultaneously following a story on TV? Do you remember you need to make a call and so you pick up your phone? If so, you are not giving the task your undivided attention, energy and focus.

We are conditioned to believe that multitasking is a valued skill, but when you spread out your energy, you water it down. You can't be a master of all things and expect great results. Focused thought will keep you on the fast track for achieving your goals, both big and small.

Identify distractions and eliminate them. As you execute any plan of action, identify what is pulling your attention away from the task at hand and then eliminate it. You may need to turn off the TV, put your cell phone in another room, or log in only to your email account and not Facebook. Even better, don't get on the Internet at all.

Eliminating distractions will initially take some discipline until it becomes a habit. Just keep in mind that distracted thoughts will not only cost you money, but your most valuable commodity: TIME!

Grand Slam and U.S. Open tennis champion Venus Williams once said, "Fifty percent of tennis is learning the strokes and being fit enough and fifty percent is how well you can control your mind in a match." The ability to focus on a goal without being distracted is what differentiates players from champions.

Monitor your progress regularly. This will ensure you are indeed on the right track, and will allow you to make corrections while you keep moving forward. If you find yourself making the same mistakes over and over again, or are remaining stagnant, it's time to change strategies or do something different. And if something isn't working at all, stop doing it!

Most people don't even realize they suffer from Scattered Thinking Syndrome. Now that you're aware of how this can sabotage your reaching your full potential, you can develop good habits to overcome STS. The trend of your life can be changed in a short amount of time just by organizing your thoughts, so think wisely!

Insight 9: Overcome "Scattered Thinking Syndrome"

Insight 10:

De-clutter!

"Three Rules of Work: Out of clutter find simplicity. From discord find harmony. In the middle of difficulty lies opportunity."

~Albert Einstein

T he condition of your physical surroundings affects every aspect of your life, including personal relationships, your health, and even your success in business. A seed can't grow if it is surrounded by weeds; similarly, people can't grow if they're surrounded by clutter. Clutter blocks the flow of positive energy and can weigh you down. Who do you think is more happy and productive--a person whose clutter consists of a couple of junk drawers and a corner of the garage or a hoarder similar to someone you might see on a popular reality show?

A cluttered physical environment translates to emotional clutter; if you have physical clutter in your home, office or vehicle, you will have clutter in your mind as well. Clutter translates into emotional baggage and the related stress drains your energy level.

It's easy to accumulate clutter. Over time, we simply collect too many things that we are not willing to let go. My father used to say, "We become a slave of our possessions."

Here are some tips to set yourself free as you start to de-clutter your life.

- **Start small.** De-cluttering is a process that can be quite overwhelming. Instead of planning to clean the entire garage, commit to organizing one section. A project broken down task by task will seem much more manageable.
- **Set a time limit.** Tell yourself you're going to work toward de-cluttering for only 20 minutes. You can do just about anything for 20 minutes! Set your kitchen timer. When your time is up, you can walk away having accomplished your goal. Chances are, however, that once you get the momentum going, you'll want to continue until the job is completed.
- **Release what no longer serves you.** Keep the best and toss the rest. Note how you feel when you hold an item. If it doesn't empower you or bring your happiness, it's time to let it go. De-clutter by selling or donating items that can be of value to someone else. Why hold on to things you will probably never use? When you let go of things that have been draining you, you will began to feel a sense of lightness and well being.
- **Visualize how you'll feel after you complete a de-cluttering task.** Think of what it feels like after you've cleaned out your car or closet when you step back and admire your work. Remember that sensation the next time you approach a de-cluttering task. Even the smallest feeling of empowerment is incentive to move you in the right direction.
- **Make de-cluttering a habit for life.** Plan to clean out your vehicle at least once a week and keep it tidy by throwing out any trash every time you get gas. Don't allow bills to pile up; set aside a regular time to pay them, and keep them organized in one place. Keep up to date on all your email—computer files create clutter, too! Never leave the house a mess. Make your bed

every morning and set a routine before you leave. Pick up any clothes on the floor and make sure the dishes are washed or in the dishwasher.

Make a conscious effort to live a clutter-free life. De-cluttering increases your energy and efficiency, gives you peace of mind, and creates space for positive change so you can fulfill your life's purpose. Having too much clutter can put your life on hold. Clear up your space and allow new positive energy to flow into your life.

Insight 10: De-clutter!

Insight 11:

Generate Enthusiasm

"Knowledge is power and enthusiasm pulls the switch."

~Steve Droke

"**N**othing great has ever been achieved without enthusiasm." Those words of wisdom came from American poet and philosopher Ralph Waldo Emerson, considered to be one of the wisest men who ever lived. I would like you to reflect on this philosophy, and here's why: Our ability to stay enthusiastic about what we do will determine the degree of our success.

How would you rate your current level of enthusiasm as it relates to your overall approach to life? Do you consider yourself to be an enthusiastic person? Do you wake up each morning with excitement, looking forward to what the day has to offer? If not, you're missing out. Enthusiasm translates to positive energy and motivation, two ingredients essential to success.

Sure, we all go through times when our level of enthusiasm takes a dip. At any given moment, there's probably something going on with you—maybe involving your finances, career, or relationship—that has the potential to leave you feeling drained and unenthusiastic. Life happens to all us, and it's important that we respond to situations with a positive attitude.

One thing we must understand is that just as machines break down, so do you humans. If a machine that has been making your life easier breaks down, you would certainly repair it. How long could you go without your washing machine? It would be much harder to wash your clothes in the creek with a rock, right?

The same principle applies to the essence of you. Life becomes much less difficult if your personal machine is working well, and one way to keep it humming along smoothly is by maintaining enthusiasm. As a start, keep in mind these tips for staying enthusiastic and positively motivated:

- **Start your day with positive thoughts and gratitude.** Think about all you are grateful for, stretch out your arms and say, "Today is a wonderful day filled with opportunity and new challenges!" or, "Each day I get better and better!" I like to play a spoken word self-development audio program first thing in the morning to fill my subconscious mind with positive thoughts and to set the tone for the day. I created an audio program called "The Reveal, Dream Big Never Quit," which is filled with positive quotes and affirmations, just for this purpose. Words have tremendous power!

- **Maintain your focus.** Identify what matters most to you and focus on those things. Remember, what you focus on gains power and what you ignore withers away. Focus on becoming better and better, and recognize what you already do well. As you push your potential and learn more about your craft, the more enthusiastic you will become. Think of how a child's enthusiasm increases as they get better at reading— you're that child now, only bigger!

- **Help others.** In conversation, think of yourself as a role model and speak accordingly. Personally, I am enthusiastic about helping others discover their hidden talents and finding what makes them happy in life. When people come to realize their life's purpose, they uncover a tremendous inflow of power. Helping others achieve their potential empowers you as well.

- **Visualize your personal squad of cheerleaders.** When I am in the gym preparing to lift weights, I picture my own personal cheering squad in front of me. They consist of people who have inspired me during my life, some of them living and some have passed. I vividly see and hear them telling me all the reasons why I can do it and how much they believe in me. This builds my enthusiasm and motivation, and I invite you to try it, too.

- **Stay present and in the moment**. When you stay in the present moment you will discover an amazing experience that will change how you deal with life's adversities. Soon after my beloved mother passed away, I was speaking with my friend Dr. Russell Hart after church service. He could sense the hurt and terrible sadness I projected, and offered advice I will never forget: "Stay present and stay positive." Dr. Hart passed away a few years after our conversation, but his words remain with me to this day. You can feel sadness or anxiety only when you think about something in the past or the future. The present is your strongest point of power, because the present moment is always perfect.

Enthusiasm can thrive only in a mind with thoughts of creating and promise. Learn to shut out any negative thoughts which may come into your mind and quickly replace them with joyful and positive ones. Remember to stay positive and present--this is the key to making every day your best day ever!

Insight 11: Generate Enthusiasm

Insight 12:

Live with Integrity

"If you have integrity, nothing else matters. If you don't have integrity, nothing else matters."

~Alan Simpson

I ntegrity is defined as the quality of having high moral principles, such as being reliable and trustworthy. It is also defined as the state of being whole and undivided; in other words, being in complete harmony with what you believe, say, and do.

Integrity forms the foundation of all relationships, both personal and in business. Integrity is the hallmark for a truly successful life because having personal integrity passes on through all your endeavors. There's no shortage of individuals who describe themselves as having integrity, but many fall prey to dishonest business practices when they give in to greed and forfeit their beliefs. This is the main reason they fail.

Having integrity is an easy and natural way to be. As you'll see in the following steps, a life of integrity is much easiest to conduct than one that constantly resists behavior in a way that goes against your inherent value system.

- **Don't necessarily follow the crowd**. People with integrity focus on what is the right thing to do, not what everyone else does. They do not allow themselves to fall prey to peer pressure like impressionable adolescents. Don't pretend to hold a point of view just because it's popular. That is the same as saying that your opinion is meaningless.

- **Live close to the truth**. The best way to conduct yourself with integrity is to live close to the truth. When someone asks you a question, don't try to second guess what it is they want to hear. This is a sure way to compromise your integrity because the best answer is always going to be the truth. This is also the easiest answer; it is much easier to speak the truth than spend energy fabricating a response.

- **Don't cut corners**. Remember, if something is worth doing, it's worth doing right. Society has conditioned us to search for the quick fix—to take a magic pill or look for shortcuts, bypassing what is required to do something the right way. This only shortchanges you as well as any possible future business or clients, which is a sure way to earn a bad reputation. You may think you are doing well in the moment or saving money in the long run; however, you're only fooling yourself.

- **Put yourself in the other person's shoes**. There is always a reason why people do what they do. A person of integrity considers the conditions and events in other people's life and how they molded them into the person they are today. When you do that, you can better treat people accordingly.

- **Never compromise your values**, even if faced with what is presented as a "golden opportunity." Someone might ask you to join their business—with the promise of lots of money and the opportunity of a lifetime—but if they ask you to do something that compromises your beliefs or standards, my answer for this is pretty simple: Don't do it! Once you compromise your moral or ethical values, you can't go back. This is one reason so many athletes, entertainers, and politicians have turned to drugs—to mask certain things they have done to get to where they are. One thing you don't want to live with is the guilt and regret of compromising your deep beliefs. It may be hard at first, considering the lure of big bucks and a life on Easy Street, but you will be filled with stress and anxiety that will continue to build over time. No amount of money or fame is worth compromising your integrity. Remember, maintaining integrity before profit will result in more profit in the long run.

- **Do the right thing**. Every time you go against the values you know are right in your heart, you compromise your integrity, which slowly erodes your self-esteem. You don't walk with your head quite as high when you've compromised your integrity. Other people can pick up on this, and may treat you differently. But what's even more important is that you will treat yourself differently.

- **Keep the promises you make**. Don't say you'll do something if you know it will be impossible to follow through. Be upfront right from the beginning about what you can do and what you can't—in other words, tell the truth! Whenever possible, under-promise and over-deliver.

- **Create a constant physical reminder of what integrity means and what you stand for**. Perhaps keep a business card style reminder in your wallet and recite it every day. Refer to do it when you feel you need it.

Living with integrity is effortless and builds peace of mind. When you live with integrity, your actions are consistently regarded as truthful. You stick to your principles and say no to acts that may demoralize your true character for what may seem to be some type of materialistic gain at the time.

It is said, "What you do daily determines your future." Imagine what your life would be like if you maintain your integrity? Your dedication to living with integrity will determine your ultimate success!

Insight 13:

Release Negative People from Your Life

"If you accept the expectations of others, especially negative ones, then you will change the outcome."

~ Michael Jordan

The people you surround yourself with--friends, relatives, co-workers and others in your social circle-- can have a huge impact on how you feel about yourself and life in general. People who have a positive outlook bolster your spirits and provide the support you need to achieve your goals. Negative people bring you down; their lack of faith in their abilities and poor sense of self-worth can easily rub off on you if you're not careful to protect yourself from their pessimism.

I want to share an encounter that one of my writer friends, Linda Lou, experienced with someone she thought was a friend. I'll let her tell the story in her own words.

****

I remember one Sunday night several years ago. I met a friend for a drink and boy, was I ready for one. I'd just come off three exhilarating, though exhausting, days at the Las Vegas Writer's Conference and was still bubbling with excitement. This was back when I was trying to interest an agent or publisher in my humorous memoir, *Bastard Husband: A Love Story.*

"I connected with two agents and an acquisitions editor who are interested in my book," I gushed. "They all want to see the first 50 pages. Isn't that great?"

My friend politely let me continue.

"Plus I taught four sessions during the conference—I got some really nice feedback—and..."

At that point he cut me off. "Wait a minute," he said, shaking his head. "Let me ask you, what have you published?" Before I could say a word, he added, "And I don't mean..."

What he didn't mean, and the answer I was poised to respond with, was the excerpt from my book that was published in an anthology of Las Vegas Valley writers. I could tell such a minor publication didn't count in his eyes.

And what he did mean--what he really wanted to say--was, "Who are you to be teaching anyone anything? You're not even published. Not really, anyway."

I took a breath and swallowed the venom on the tip of my tongue.

"I know where you're going with that question," I calmly replied. "The sessions were on technical writing, how to track your agent queries, and how to get the most out of the conference. I actually know a little something about those topics." My answer satisfied him, but I seethed for quite a while longer.

I can't think of another time when I went from elation to deflation in such a flash, though I'm reminded of a boyfriend I once had who, whenever I mentioned any glimmer of optimism surrounding my book, would invariably respond with, "I hate to see you get your hopes up." He hated to see me get my hopes up? What is an artist without hope??? Needless to say, he wasn't my boyfriend for long.

There's a lesson here for all of us who are writers, artists, musicians, or other creative types: We have to be careful who we hang out with. We face enough rejection in our artistic pursuits; we sure as hell don't need our friends (or relatives) tainting our energy fields with doubt and negativity. I'm not saying they're bad people; they just don't understand. And I'm willing to bet they either have no artistic inclination themselves, or just as likely, they did at one time and someone (probably their parents) rewarded them the same skepticism they're now passing on to us.

The point is, we can't expect these people to be a source of encouragement. Rather than risk having to defend our dreams, it's best to not even bring them up. Restrict the conversation to the weather. Better to identify your kindred spirits and share your successes and challenges with them instead.

Sometimes it's in your best interest to let some relationships fizzle out.

****

Yes, sometimes it's in your best interest to release certain individuals from your life. Don't think of it as being mean; you're actually doing yourself a favor. You have to respect yourself enough to let these people go. Of course, there are some people--family members, for instance--who we're pretty much stuck with. In that case, it's important to recognize their negativity for what it is and not let it penetrate your psyche or impede your determination to succeed.

Who knows? Maybe your fortitude and desire for achievement will rub off on them. We can only hope.

As for my friend Linda, she had the last laugh. Her memoir was published and she even had a one-woman show in Las Vegas based on her book. She has not seen her friend since that encounter.

Insight 14:

Reposition and Empower Yourself

"Start early and begin raising the bar throughout the day."

~Bruce Jenner

W hat does anyone really want out of life? More life, of course! As long as it's a happy life, right? We all have the same goal: to be happy. And in order to live a happy life, we must feel empowered. When we are empowered, we feel energetic and have the vitality and zest we need to fulfill our purpose in life.

So many people work their whole lives at a job they can barely tolerate. They look forward to—no, they *live for—* retirement. "Once I retire," they say, "that's when life will begin!" Yet in the process, they're not really living; they're just marking time until they reach that defined point somewhere in the future. They have no personal power in the present.

Retirement should not be looked at as freedom. No, freedom is something we should feel our entire lives, no matter what. If you are stuck in a job that saps your energy and drains your soul, get unstuck. Reposition yourself. Put your resume together and search for a job that is more in line with your natural talents; something you'll enjoy doing.

But maybe you feel it would be unwise to make a career move at this time. Let's say you're in a job you do not like very much, but for now it makes sense because it pays the bills until you get through school or until you're in a better position to find a job you're passionate about. In the meantime, try to frame your current job in a way that you can live with it. Look for and focus on the positive aspects of it. Before you walk into your workplace each day, think of how grateful you are to have a job. Realize that your current position will help you transition to your next goal in life. Think of how one day you can inspire others by sharing your road to success. Find the time *after* work to do things that fuel your passion and uplift your enthusiasm for living.

Repositioning yourself is a personal responsibility; no one can do it for you. The first step in repositioning is to recognize what is not working in your life. What, exactly, is not going the way you would like? How far are you now from where you would like to be? What needs to happen to get you closer to that point? What concrete steps can you take to get there?

The key is to always move in the direction that feels best. For example, if you live in a part of the country that rains constantly and you feel depressed by the rain, then move someplace sunny. Okay, that may be easier said than done. But if you can't move to another part of the country, maybe you can move into a house with more natural lighting. Or add better lighting to your current house to give the feeling of brightness. If you're out of shape physically, figure out what it would take to get yourself in shape. Don't join a gym if you know you hate going to the gym—identify the activities that you wouldn't mind doing and then do them.

Who do you know who might have similar interests when it comes to fitness or the other goals you are working to attain? Engage those people to join you, or at least make it a point to spend more time with them. I have one particular friend whose zest and energy for life shines through like a fully charged battery. Every time we speak, she puts me in that same fully charged zone and I'm ready to take on the world.

You see, just by setting that example, we can help others feel empowered. And when we help others, we empower ourselves as well. Yes, it's that simple! Haven't you ever noticed how good you feel when you do something nice for someone? So search out opportunities to pass on good thoughts and actions to others every chance you get!

Understand that we can correct only what we are willing to confront. We must make the decision that enough is enough, and do whatever it takes to make the change. Don't let fear stand in your way. Some people have a fear of failure, a fear of the unknown, or are afraid that their hard work will never pay off. Whatever the reason, there's no excuse. You must remind yourself constantly why you want to make the changes that will reposition yourself and empower your life. The simple answer is, "You're worth it."

Learn to cultivate a passion and a reason for everything you do, even if it may be undesirable at the time. Always do your best. This builds character and prepares you for bigger and better things to come. No matter what your age, by repositioning yourself you will empower your life with the happiness you deserve.

Insight 14: Reposition and Empower Yourself

Insight 15:

Ask Questions

"The art and science of asking questions is the source of all knowledge."

~Thomas Berger

N obel Prize recipient Naguib Mahfouz said, "You can tell if a man is clever by his answers. You can tell if a man is wise by his questions." Throughout history, people who have been successful in business and in life in general all have one thing in common: They tend to ask good questions, and they are not afraid to ask.

The art of asking questions is an important life skill. Questions can have tremendous power when asked properly. They can be used to solve just about any problem you may have. Doctors ask questions to determine their patients' diagnoses. Attorneys ask questions to determine guilt or innocence. Politicians ask for votes. Someone who was once broke asked, "How do I become rich?" Learning to ask the right questions of the right people can have a tremendous impact on both your business and personal life.

The problem is many people do not know what questions to ask; therefore, they will never obtain the knowledge they are looking for. They may feel a sort of paralysis driven by the fear of being rejected or the fear of looking stupid. Fear, however, is never an ingredient for success.

Here are some guidelines for overcoming the fear of asking questions, as well as a couple of other nuggets of information.

- **If you want something, don't be afraid to ask for it.** Over the years I've cultivated the habit of asking for what I want and it's helped me tremendously. If you never ask, the answer will always be "no." Musician Billy Joel was giving a lecture/performance at Vanderbilt University when a fan asked if he could accompany him on the piano. Joel paused for a couple of seconds and then said, "Okay," no doubt giving the fan the biggest thrill of his life. Would that ever have happened had the fan been consumed by fear?

- **Don't be afraid to ask for advice.** Human beings have an inborn desire to help others. By asking for advice, you recognize the person as an authority. People are flattered to be in a position to give advice and by the fact that someone thinks their opinion has value. What would you say if someone approached you with, "I have a very important project and can really use your expertise. Will you please help me?" I have a feeling you'd respond with a resounding, "Yes!"

- **Don't be afraid to seek out the experts.** Why not approach the best in the field? You might be surprised at their willingness to help. Successful people who remember where they came from will also remember when they, too, asked for help. A true class act will be happy to pay it forward.

- **Don't be afraid to look stupid.** If you need clarification or more information, ask for it! We can learn an important lesson from children, who ask a question and then follow up with "Why?" until they are satisfied. They don't do that to be a pain; they're simply looking for greater understanding. As children we were full of questions, seeking answers to new discoveries. Somehow as we got older, we got the impression that we will appear to be stupid if we ask the wrong question, so we refrain from asking anything at all. But how smart is that?

- **Don't ask questions just to satisfy your curiosity.** I know a man who is 7 feet tall and he can't go *anywhere* without people asking, "How tall are you?" He hears this question several times a day every day of his life. What difference does his height make to anyone? Before asking personal questions, consider your motivation. Don't bother someone because you just "need to know."

- **Ask questions of yourself.** For example, as you climb your ladder to success, one of the best questions you can ask yourself is, "What is the next action I can take that will contribute to my success?" Questions you ask of yourself can be very empowering.

Learning to ask questions well can have dramatic results with your business as well as personal life. It can take years off your learning curve—think of how much easier it is to ask someone a question rather than research the answer yourself. Your goals can be reached in record time. So forget about fear--just ask!

Insight 16:

Give and Receive Appreciation

"Appreciation is a wonderful thing: It makes what is excellent in others belong to us as well."

~Voltaire

Think about it, why do we value close friends and family? Why do we feel pleased when others say, "Thank you" or "Great job"? Because it is a wonderful thing to feel loved and appreciated.

Mother Theresa, famed humanitarian and limitless thinker, once said, "There is more hunger for love and appreciation in this world than for bread." If this statement is true—and I believe it is—then our need for love and appreciation is above all other human needs since it's the most important form of nourishment for life.

It is so very important to show appreciation for others. Unexpressed appreciation is useless. No good comes from it if the person is not recognized for who they are and the work they do. One study has shown that 46% of people quit their jobs due to lack of appreciation. And you can be certain that many relationships, both personal and in business, have been destroyed for the same reason.

Additionally, the expression of authentic appreciation creates a sense of well-being for both sides. Highly effective leaders in the workplace recognize the impact of sincere appreciation and recognition on productivity. Recognition inspires optimism and passion; people who are recognized for a job well done feel recharged and eager to do more.

I have personally experienced the power of appreciation in business. Years ago I was having trouble adjusting to a new workplace, so I wrote a heartfelt letter to the president of the company explaining my concerns and expressing my appreciation for having been given such a great opportunity. Soon after, I received a very understanding response, which motivated me to do the best job I possibly could. I increased my personal productivity, which of course had a positive impact on the company's bottom line.

Because of the appreciation from their supporters, many world leaders, humanitarians and innovators have gained momentum and passion for the pursuit of excellence. This is important because the fact is, there is no such thing as a self-made man. Every "picture of success" achieved what they did with the help of others backing them along the way. When a player makes a winning touchdown in a championship game, most people give credit to that one person, yet he couldn't have done it alone. This is why it's always important to recognize those who may not be in the spotlight and let them know how much you appreciate their efforts.

Knowing how powerful appreciation is, take a moment to think about how you express appreciation to others. On a scale of 1 to 10, how would you rate yourself? Think of the people with whom you've come in contact in the past few days— the waitress who served you in the coffee shop, the trash collector you nodded to on your way to work, even the police officer who gave you a ticket—did you tell them you appreciate them?

Instead of focusing on someone's faults, praise them for their strengths and the potential you see in them. You have to remember that in everything around us there is both good and bad, and by focusing on the good we will attract more positive energy. Be genuine and creative when showing someone appreciation and recognition. Don't just tell them what a wonderful job they did, but let them know you really mean it by saying something specific about how it made your life better. Always address the person by their first name; it's the sweetest sound they will ever hear. This will make a world of difference. Another great way to show appreciation is through a handwritten letter or personalized thank you card.

And let's not forget to show appreciation for yourself! When was the last time you acknowledged just how magnificent you are? Always remember to celebrate yourself, whether it's with a well-deserved vacation, massage, or even just taking some "me" time. The key to applying the wonderful power of appreciation begins with focusing on the good of others *as well as yourself.*

Always remember the feeling you get when you are appreciated by others, and always pay that feeling forward!

Insight 16: Give and Receive Appreciation

Insight 17:

Master the Art of Accelerated Learning

"Live as if you were to die tomorrow. Learn as if you were to live forever."

~Mahatma Gandhi

One particular quality world class leaders seem to have in common is they learn in the fastest, most efficient manner so they can apply that knowledge in their business and personal lives immediately.

In my workshops, I teach techniques that instill positive changes in behavior. To meet my training objectives, I must deliver information in a way that my students will not only comprehend, but retain so they can implement the knowledge gained into their lives.

I use what is known as accelerated learning techniques, which encompass a wide variety of teaching methods and media. I may have my students acknowledge certain phrases I say by verbally answering "yes" or "no," or I may repeat key points several times and have my students write them down and repeat them out loud. Simply asking them questions is another instructional technique.

But can you increase learning on your own? The answer is absolutely yes! However, you must take the initiative to invest your time and master the art of accelerated learning.

There are literally thousands of techniques you can use to improve your learning and retention. These insights take practice, and not all of these may be for you. My intention is to present you with a choice. Here are some of the techniques that have worked for me.

- **Speed reading.** Learning to read faster with full comprehension is a skill that has been mastered by world class leaders. The late United States president John F. Kennedy developed his reading speed to 1,200 words per minute, and former president Jimmy Carter, along with former first lady Rosalynn Carter, would have speed reading classes inside the White House and allow their staff members to attend. George Washington was also known to be a speed reader.

- **Taking a good speed reading course can be of great benefit.** In the meantime, this simple, yet powerful trick can help you double your reading speed: Place your finger below the line you are reading in the center of the page, instead of under each word. This prevents your eyes from wandering around the page, and reduces eye strain and time spent reading. Give it a shot!

- **Automatic learning.** One of my favorite learning techniques is to play an educational audio program as I am falling asleep. Adjust the sound so it is just loud enough where you can barely hear it, but you can still understand the words. I have found this to have amazing results. Just relax without giving the program much attention and allow yourself to drift asleep. All the information you hear will seep into your subconscious.

- **This is also good to do as soon as you wake up**. I have produced audio programs with structured musical compositions in the background of spoken positive messages. Playing these audio programs when doing chores or driving works wonders for feeding this information into your subconscious mind, even if you're not paying special attention to them. You can even create your own audio program customized with the content you want to learn.

- **Note taking**. This technique helps you recall important information long after you first hear it. It's a good idea to get in the habit of relentlessly taking notes, even for information you may already be familiar with. Whether I'm at a seminar, movie, reading a book, or sitting in a classroom, I always take notes to remember something I just heard or learned, or to capture new ideas that pop into my head. I never leave it to memory. I like to take initial notes on my cell phone's note pad, on a napkin or in a notebook, and then rewrite the ideas into a Word document. When possible, record the learning session so you can replay it over and over to feed your subconscious mind.

- **Total immersion learning.** With this technique you do nothing but eat, sleep, and breathe your subject matter. Once I was studying for a very important state exam and for three weeks prior, that exam consumed my life. I studied in class. I played audio programs on my iPod. I meditated and created my own mantras such as, "All the answers flow to me easily..." Surround yourself with everything about the subject you're learning and you can't help but retain it.

To facilitate learning, follow these three tips:

1. Periodically take a deep breath. Relax and remove any tension and distractions. Focus on the learning task at hand and nothing else.

2. Pace your learning. Your brain needs down time. You can try to read a difficult book for eight hours straight, but after a while, how much of the information will you retain?

75

3. Create a structure for learning. Do this as you would plan a work day. Block out a time and a specific study place, such as the public library, where you'll be free from distractions. Turn your cell phone off. Make an appointment to get together with a study buddy so you will be obligated to show up. If you are both studying the same subject, have a pow-wow after each session to discuss what you have learned and to hold each other accountable for any study goals.

Discover the process that works best for you. When you make a conscious decision to accelerate your learning, you can awaken dormant talents, build a new career, and accomplish goals you once only dreamed of.

Go the extra mile and become a learning leader. Remember, there are no traffic jams on the extra mile!

Insight 18:

Develop a Mental Fitness Regimen

"Remember your brain is involved in everything you do."

~ Dr. Daniel G. Amen

O ne of the first steps for personal empowerment is to align your mind and body to work at their optimal levels. The two certainly work together; if we take care of our minds, our minds will take care of our bodies and vice versa. However, I believe fitness begins with the mind.

Why? Because the body is controlled by the brain. The brain is the organizer of the body. Whatever will help the brain will help the rest of the body, and the energy factor of the body depends on a healthy brain. If the brain begins to deteriorate, it can no longer give the body proper direction. When that happens, internal organs no longer function properly. This can result in serious health consequences, even death.

To keep your mind strong, you must constantly use it. Like the body, you must "use it or lose it." Anything that lacks stimulation will stop working and eventually wither away and die. This goes for every body part and organ including eyesight, hearing, muscles, as well as your brain.

Stimulating the mind is the key to keeping it healthy. By doing that, you can tap into your limitless reserves of creativity, which serves as a catalyst for unleashing our life's potential.

Let's look at some exercises and strategies to keep your mind alert and your body strong.

- **Take a fun approach to solving a problem**. Think of something you'd like to change and then brainstorm as many possible solutions as you can. Allow yourself to "think outside the box," with no idea being too crazy or unrealistic. Try to come up with at least 25 possible alternatives. When you're done, review the ideas you've generated. Chances are at least one or two will actually work!

- **Come up with an invention**. Again, don't limit your thinking. Write down all your ideas for a new product in the greatest detail you can. Draw pictures of it. You just might end up taking it to market.

- **Play a memory boosting game**. Remember the old TV show *Concentration*? Create a similar game by spreading out a deck of cards in front of you, all face down. Then flip two cards up for each turn. The object is to turn over pairs of matching cards. This is a great game to play with young children, though people of any age will find it challenging and stimulating.

- **Listen to soothing, structured music.** Studies have shown that listening to composers such as Mozart helps to increase concentration levels.

- **Learn something new.** Learning challenges your brain and helps boost memory power. Choose from over 2000 high quality online courses offered through www.Lynda.com for only a very reasonable fee. Or check out www.coursera.org and take online college courses offered by leading universities such as Duke, Columbia, and John Hopkins for *free*!

- **Use your non-dominant hand.** Doing the same thing over and over can make your brain lazy. Perform a mundane task with the opposite hand. For example, if you're right handed, brush your teeth using your left hand. This will stimulate the opposite side of your brain.
- **Get your blood pumping.** The brain depends on a healthy blood supply, and cardiovascular exercise such as walking, running, or swimming can help you optimize your brain's functioning.
- **Start the day nutritionally smart.** I personally like to be creative. I add some milled flax seed to my oatmeal for omega 3, and sometimes throw in some blueberries for antioxidants and flavor. Your brain can use a protein lift after several hours of sleeping, so eggs or chicken would be a good choice. Eliminate simple carbohydrates such white flour and sugars. This will optimize your brain for the day and increase performance. And don't forget the best supplement in the world: water. Keep hydrated!
- **Work on your brain while working on your body.** When walking on a treadmill your brain can become disengaged, so listen to a language learning program, inspirational talk or music to keep your mind stimulated.
- **Get a good night's sleep.** Never underestimate the importance of sleep. Early to bed and early to rise will keep your brain sharp and wise.

Make taking care of your mind your number priority now. Combining mental exercise, physical exercise, and nutrition into your fitness regimen can enhance your total performance and lead you to a much more productive life. Find the stimulation techniques that work best for you. Be creative and remember to have fun doing it!

Insight 18: Develop a Mental Fitness Regimen

Insight 19:

Build a Successful Business

"Successful companies create value by providing products or services their customers value more highly than available alternatives. Value creation involves making peoples' lives better. It is contributing to prosperity in society."

~Charles Koch

I've enjoyed the benefits of building not one, but several successful businesses. I've enjoyed being in control of my own income, as well as the growing the business as much or as little as I wanted. One of the benefits of having your own business is that if you build it correctly with a proper structure, many options are available to you. You can retire when you want, start another business, sell the business, or even franchise it.

This year thousands of new businesses will open for the first time, fueled by the enthusiasm of entrepreneurship. However, in a few short years, most of those businesses will no longer be in operation. That will be a disappointment not only for the business owners, but for their employees who will find themselves without jobs.

To help ensure success and prevent your business from being a statistic in the casualty column, here are some key principles and processes to follow when undertaking the challenge of opening a new business.

- **Understand that your value is in your difference.** Follow what I call "The Golden Principle." It goes like this: *The responsibility and purpose of a business is to satisfy customers by offering them goods and services of real value.* Please memorize that. It's important because if you hold true to it, you will succeed 100% of the time. What do I mean by "real value" when it comes to your business? Your value is in your difference. For example, let's say there are two apples in front of you. Although they may look similar, one is more expensive than the other. Which would you buy? Probably the less expensive one. Now, if I were to explain that the higher priced apple was grown without the use of pesticides in special fields on an organic farm and had much higher nutritional value than the other apple, which was grown with nasty chemicals that could cause you harm, which one would you choose? I hope you would opt for the higher priced, healthier apple. Why? Because although it's priced higher, you now understand the value is better, so it's actually less expensive. Similarly, sometimes you have to explain value to the customer by describing what differentiates your product or service from others. This may involve sharing the process behind the product as well as the short- and long-term benefits.
- **Keep up with technological innovations**. We are living in a world of exponential growth. Things you learn today may be much different or obsolete a year from now. Stay ahead of the game by constantly updating your business knowledge. What you don't know can hurt you. Therefore, learn everything about your market, your services, and your products--more

than anyone else on the planet. Think of how evolving technologies will change the way you'll do business. How will you keep up?

- **Listen to the public.** Sadly, many people go into business having done very little information gathering. Make sure your product or service meets the market demands by conducting some research. Test a pool of consumers in both your target market and across different demographics to determine and gage public interest. When you perform your due diligence, your chances for success increase dramatically.

- **Be the general!** Building a business is like playing a game of strategy. The word *strategy* comes from the Greek work *strategos*, which means general, as in a military general. When it comes to running a business, you are the general. You develop the strategy and control all that goes on into your business by taking charge and staying on top of every area of operation. Although you may delegate certain jobs to employees or partners, it's up to you to make sure the organization is running smoothly. Never assume that everything's fine; a lot can go wrong when you are not watching. Check for weak links and rotten apples. Find problems and address them quickly.

- **Prepare and immerse yourself completely.** There is absolutely no substitute for preparation. You must also go into this endeavor with commitment, dedication, and the full belief that your efforts will be fruitful. Monitor your progress, and make sure you're constantly moving forward. Always look for areas to improve.

- **Be specific in identifying your purpose and path.** Be so precise that when someone asks you what your business is about, the words flow from your mouth with confidence and conviction. Know exactly what you want, why you want it, and how you will get there. When asked how you differentiate yourself from your competitors, never answer with, "We provide better customer service." Everybody says that, and most do not deliver it. Instead, give specifics. Talk about your process, your ingredients, your training and, of course, your value.

- **Keep your business front and center in the public's mind.** Send your customers personal thank you notes, the old fashioned kind they can hold in their hands. I always say, "Brighten someone's mailbox, instead of their inbox." Also keep them informed of new information about your business, and make sure it's relevant to their needs. Keep your business energy alive, at the forefront of your customers' minds. It's important to advertise, and when you build a good solid business with a wonderful reputation, you get the best form of advertising for free: word of mouth!

- **Be nice**. People do business with people they like, it's that simple. People like people who are friendly, genuinely pleasant and sincere, and easy to talk with. Good chemistry is crucial, especially when you're providing a service.

We may never discover the meaning of life; however, you can discover the purpose of your life. Building a successful business that fulfills an unmet need can be a rewarding way to express your purpose. Find something you are passionate about--that passion will give you the enthusiasm needed to keep persevering toward success.

Insight 20:

Be the CEO of Your Own Life

"Do your work with your whole heart and you will succeed. There is so little competition."

~Elbert Hubbard

S uppose you were paying someone a lot of money to manage your life. Considering how things are going right now, should that person still have a job?

If the answer is no, then you need to fire that person. But wait… *you're* the person managing your life, right? Since you can't fire yourself, you'll have to fire your current way of thinking and start managing your life the way the world's most successful CEOs run their businesses. It's time you discover the power of purposeful planning and strategic project management and apply these practices to the things that matter most to you.

Let's put it this way: If someone gave you a project to do at work, you would do it or you'd be out of a job. You would meet each milestone along the way and according to the timeline established by your project manager. If you were falling behind, you'd work overtime to meet the deadline.

Project management applies to your personal life as well. Every goal you set for yourself is a project, and you're the project manager. It's up to you to create the project plan. It's up to you to set the timeline for when things need to be done. It's up to you to work overtime as required to make sure everything goes according to plan.

In other words, you must approach the projects of your life with the same diligence you would if you were at work. Think about it—why would you put more effort into someone else's goals than your own? Who are you ultimately working for? If you don't design your own life plan, chances are you'll fall into someone else's plan. And guess what they have planned for you? Not much.

Whether or not you have experience managing projects at work, you're still the CEO of your own life. Here are some things to consider when creating a strategic and purposeful plan that can take your goals from an idea to reality.

- **Begin by having a clear vision of what you want and the purpose that goal will serve.** You must see it, and you must believe you can achieve it. Think limitlessly! Allow yourself to imagine how your life would be without self-imposed limitations.

- **Write a detailed list of each step that must be taken in order to achieve the goal.** It's important to put this list on paper. It's much easier to tell what needs to be done when you're looking at a list in front of you, as opposed to trying to manage everything in your head. A written list will empty your mind and prevent your brain from becoming overloaded. Be sure to prioritize your list and check items off as you go.

- **Identify the tasks you can delegate, as well as the areas that will require the expertise of others.** Look for and develop a positive circle of influence, and surround yourself with competent individuals. Choose your team carefully; individuals with undesirable work ethics will be perceived as a reflection of you. An entire organization can go down because of only one bad apple.

- **Develop the discipline needed to get the job done.** Keep in mind the principle of TNT, which stands for "today, not tomorrow." Putting off your plan is only postponing your fulfillment in life. Never put off for tomorrow what you can bring to life today. Remember, just by starting, you're half done!

- **Take notes along the way.** Don't think you'll remember every detail of your project. A lovely Chinese proverb says, "The palest ink is better than the best memory." I can't begin to tell you how many meetings, presentations or conference I attended where I was the only person taking notes. These notes can be invaluable when you refer back to them, and can make the difference between success and failure.

- **Seek inspiration and expertise from those who have done it before.** Chances are whatever your goal, someone has written a book about how to achieve it. Take advantage of the literally thousands of priceless treasures available for free courtesy of your local public library. These stories serve as proof that it can be done, and show how you can pave and follow your own road to success.

Whatever your goals are, remember the old saying, "Failing to plan is planning to fail."

The fact is, you can't achieve anything worthwhile in life unless you have a well-defined plan. Without one, the only path you're on is one that leads to stress, anxiety and failure. However, with proper planning, you'll enjoy more productivity and the peace of mind. You'll be able to recognize obstacles ahead of you and strategize how to address them. You'll enjoy improved focus, a stream of new insights and ideas, and increased confidence. You'll also develop the discipline needed to fulfill your goals.

Insight 21:

Act Like a True Leader

"If your actions inspire others to dream more, learn more, do more and become more, you are a leader."

~ John Quincy Adams

C ontrary to what the business journals might lead you to believe, you don't have to be the chief executive officer of a global conglomerate in order to be a leader. No, leaders can be found anywhere. One day I was at a fast food restaurant and noticed one particular employee who stood out among the rest. She was very attentive to the customers, smiling and offering the type of customer service beyond the expectations of what we have been accustomed to in that type of establishment. I even witnessed two separate customers giving her a tip—*in a fast food restaurant*! This woman stood out because she did not let her current position dictate her actions; instead, she allowed her genuine integrity to shine. I have no doubt that someday this employee will be a force to be reckoned with.

Leading is not just about directing the actions of others; it's about taking on the responsibility to be true to your integrity, never compromising who you are and what you stand for, and

89

conducting yourself in a manner that will inspire others. *That* is the key to leadership.

Whatever you do in life—whether you're a CEO, manager, supervisor, line employee, or a stay at home parent—your ability to lead will greatly influence the results you see in both business and your personal life. To make the most of this innate power, here are my Top 10 "must have" characteristics of a true leader:

1. A true leader accepts full responsibility personally as well as for the entire team. True leaders are willing to admit when they are wrong just as they take credit when they are right.

2. A true leader focuses on finding the best resolution for a problem and in completing the task in the fastest, most efficient manner.

3. A true leader gains the respect of others and inspires them to work toward a common goal. True leaders never look down on anyone, and instill the understanding that "We're all in this together."

4. Genuine integrity encompasses the thoughts and actions of all true leaders. They understand that success results only when they put forth the correct action accompanied by honesty and forthrightness.

5. A true leader is willing to ask for support from others, and does not play the ego game. A smart man knows what he doesn't know and isn't afraid to seek and leverage the expertise of others. True leaders are more concerned with what will work than how they would be perceived if they asked for help.

6. A true leader knows to promote the natural strengths of other individuals in order to achieve the best results. He or she clarifies roles and responsibilities so that each person

understands how they are making the organization more successful.

7. A true leader understands that just because something is offered, you don't have to say yes.

8. A true leader is deliberate in allowing others into his or her life. This type of person is slow to hire workers and is quick to fire those who do not meet expectations. They are adept at recognizing the bad seed of the group and waste no time eliminating them from their circle of influence.

9. A true leader knows how to create a work environment that is conducive to productivity and success. He or she understands the importance of organization, good quality air, and adequate lighting in order to keep the brain and body functioning well.

10. A true leader can attract talented people who are eager to work for them. A staff of enthusiastic high-performers cannot help but increase productivity, which drives the success of the organization as a whole.

When you practice these characteristics of leadership, you will begin to attract other great people who want to work with you, no matter what your endeavors are in building both your personal and business power. Remember, like attracts like, and great leaders attract great people!

Insight 21: Act Like a True Leader

Insight 22:

Change Your Life with a Four-Letter Word: Zeal

"Zeal will do more than knowledge."

~ William Hazlitt

Most people can be divided into two groups: those who manage their problems and those who are managed *by* their problems. People who allow their problems to control their lives, instead of taking control of their problems, live by default.

When "just getting by" becomes a primary objective, most individuals tend to accept what is. They figure whatever happens, happens and so they sabotage themselves from enjoying a truly fulfilled life. They write off the big dreams they once held dear and convince themselves that those dreams simply weren't in the cards for them. If you ask me, that's just sad.

The major difference that separates these two groups boils down to one incredibly magical four-letter word: *ZEAL!* Although not very commonly used in conversation, zeal is referred to throughout the Bible, and is responsible for the success of all the greatest achievers this world has ever known. Simply put, those who have zeal relentlessly pursue their goals with intense dedication, passion, energy, and enthusiasm. As I like to say, zeal sets your *desire on fire!*

Think of your zeal as the essential core of what you are, what you we're born to do, your personal branding. You should be able to express your zeal in two words or less. For example, if I mention Donald Trump, you think "real estate." William Shakespeare? "Playwright." Other example of individuals who have demonstrated tremendous zeal include Richard Branson, Nelson Mandela, Bill Gates, Alexander Bell and Leonardo da Vinci. We all know of these amazing individuals because they lived with zeal.

To help identify your zeal, ask yourself two simple questions:

1. What brings me joy or excites me?

2. What is one the one thing I want to accomplish between now and the end of my life?

It's possible to change your zeal's direction throughout your lifetime. You may have heard of a famous fashion model who left the industry to devote her life to a charity, or a business executive who gave it all up to start his own farm. Or maybe you recognize the name Rich Franklin, a mild mannered high school math teacher who quit his job and went on to become an ultimate fighter champion. I personally knew a casino executive of many years who walked away to become a full-time soccer coach. He has never been happier.

You may be someone who discovers their zeal later in life, perhaps while enjoying your retirement years. If that's the case, you're in good company. Anna Mary Robertson, better known as Grandma Moses, one of America's most successful folk artists, started painting at the age of 78. Millie Garfield was also 78 when she started blogging, an expression of her zeal, and became one of the Internet's most successful bloggers.

All of these individuals all had the courage to switch from a "play it safe" mentality to a spirit of adventure. They had the willingness to commit to living their zeal. And as you can see, it's never too late! Going after your zeal and living it is an amazing energy generator, so start working toward it now.

- **Make the time to pursue your zeal**. You can find success in anything if you are committed to taking the time to make it happen.
- **Develop a respect for all things lacking in your life; this increases your zeal**. For example, if you lack finances, develop respect for finances. If you lack fitness, develop a respect for fitness.
- **Consider all the natural talents you possess, and never underestimate their true value and power.**
- **Visualize yourself already living your zeal.** Form mental images and reinforce them with affirmations. Meditate each day on your vision, and know it's on its way to you.

This world needs what we all have to offer. So many ideas and inventions remain undiscovered when people choose not to live out their zeal—whether they give in to inertia or self-doubt or negativity instilled by others. Think of how your ideas and purpose can benefit others. I often tell people that if you neglect to act on an idea that can help yourself as well as benefit the lives of others, you are being selfish.

So if you are not already living your zeal, it's time to get moving and *"Get your zeal on."* The power of zeal is tremendous. When you find something that gives you great zeal, suddenly excuses and doubt disappear and you plow through obstacles like water through sand. Be bold. Stop waiting for the approval of others. In the words of Benjamin Franklin, a true man of zeal, "Never leave till tomorrow that can be done today. He who hesitates is lost."

Insight 22: Change Your Life with a Four-Letter Word: Zeal

Insight 23:

Create an Efficient and Inspiring Home Office

"Efficiency is intelligent laziness."

~David Dunham

W orking out of a home office offers a multitude of benefits including flexible work hours, a potential tax write-off, and no commuting time or associated costs. But sometimes working at home can be lonely, and the lack of personal contact with others can be less than motivating.

It makes sense that the better you feel, the better you work. Therefore, create an inspiring workspace that will bring out your best and maximize your productivity. Your home office should blend in with the rest of your living space, but still maintain its boundaries so that you are not distracted by what's going on in other areas in your home. Whatever design elements you choose, the goal is to facilitate workflow through a setup that is functional as well as attractive.

As a self-development trainer who works out of my house, I recognize the importance of a properly laid out home office. A home office should promote creative thinking, instill clarity, and provide a sense of well-being that embraces your strengths. To optimize your home office environment, follow these simple strategies:

- **Define your sources of inspiration.** Surround yourself with things that make you feel good. Decorate your workspace with a poster of a favorite quote or a photo that touches your heart. Think about the colors that make you feel alive and energized, and integrate those colors into your décor. Get rid of anything that brings you down.

- **Clear your desk.** The less you have on your desk, the better. Make the most of your work space and minimize distractions by keeping only the essentials on the surface of your work area. These might include a phone, computer, mouse, pen, and notebook. Place miscellaneous office supplies that you use only once in a while, such as paperclips and staplers, in a nearby drawer. Do not to allow papers to pile up. Order creates comfort, so "File it, don't pile it." Keep cords and cables out of view as much as possible; they only add to your sense of clutter.

- **Think life!** Houseplants not only brighten your day, but they clean the air as well. In my home office I have a live bamboo plant, which I truly enjoy.

- **Appeal to your sense of sound.** Think of the sounds that inspire you. Maybe you like the sound of the ocean or falling rain. Or maybe you get more done with classical music or punk rock playing in the background. Fill your office with sounds you enjoy, but make sure that they don't interrupt your work.

- **Organize your papers so that you can quickly find them**. Have a place for everything and put everything in its place. To find whatever you need more readily, use see-through folders or colored file folders. The colors will help them stand out and help you locate files easily.

- **Lighting is everything!** The more natural lighting, the better. If you don't have a window, or when you need artificial light, buy soft light bulbs and consider installing a dimmer switch.
- **Invest in the proper equipment.** Having the proper equipment can make a huge impact on your productivity. Consider buying an ergonomically correct office chair to protect your back and help prevent fatigue and muscle aches. This will enable you to work longer hours. If your desktop allows, add a second monitor to your computer system. Once you get used to the dual monitor setup, you'll never want to go back to a single screen--you'll enjoy the larger and more flexible visual work area way too much!

The benefits of an efficient and inspiring home office include increased productivity, creativity an enhanced sense of well-being, and job satisfaction. An efficient home office allows freedom and flexibility for you to grow and succeed. Remember, your environment can make or break you, so make your home office count, with lots of love and inspiration!

Insight 23: Create an Efficient and Inspiring Home Office

Insight 24:

Be of Service to Others

"Service to others is the rent you pay for your room here on earth."

~Muhammad Ali

W hy are some people more successful than others? Does anyone know the true secret of success?

Ask ten different people how success is obtained and you'll get ten different answers. Yes, education is important, hard work is important, talent is important. However, true success comes when we have the ability to understand what people really want and how to supply it to them. Our ability to please others through service is crucial for achieving success.

I run my life on the philosophy that if I help other people achieve their goals I am, in turn, helping myself achieve my own goals. I also use this philosophy to run my business. Whatever business you are in—whether you're a business owner, manager or an employee—your ultimate goal is to help your customers achieve their goals. We are all in the service industry! By using this strategy for business, you will attract more clients as well as get more repeat clients. Trust me, this is the smartest thing you can do for your business. And the best part is, the service-based, goal-fulfilling process starts a chain reaction that can permeate all of society.

For example, by playing music, musicians give themselves joy and they also fulfill their listeners' goal of enjoying an entertaining night out. Their audience, in turn, feels pleasant and inspired to achieve their own goals, which will benefit other people down the line.

"Life is like a game of tennis; the player who serves well seldom loses." Devoting your life to serving others is a win-win situation. Reflect on your life, and the positive impact one individual may have had on you. Think of what you can do to affect someone else's life in a positive way.

Here are some tips to help you cultivate the devotion to serving others.

- **Welcome the opportunity to learn about other people.** Be open minded to their needs and desires. Find out about their cultural background, business, family, goals, hobbies, and what they treasure most. Show sincere interest in them so you know how to best serve them in the future.
- **Always look for the best in a person**. Embrace the little idiosyncrasies that make people interesting individuals. Instead of making them feel different, make them feel important. People express their individuality in different ways, and that's their right, just as it's your right. Celebrate diversity!
- **Ask your customers which traits of exceptional service they value most and then make it a point to deliver them.** Don't forget to ask your internal customers, the people you serve within your organization, as well. Listen intently to their needs.
- **Inspire others with your friendship**. Offer help and compassion in times of struggle, and rejoice when good fortune comes their way. Show that you care and they will pass that goodness on to someone else.

- **Small gestures have a great power that can brighten someone's day.** Return a phone call, a smile, or a thank you. Hold the door or elevator.
- **Make the effort to surpass expectations.** For example, if you are a Realtor and are showing a home to a family with children, bring along some crayons and coloring books for the kids. What can you do in your personal or work life to exceed the expectations of others?
- **Approach each day as if it's the most important day of your life.** Also, treat others as if it's the most important day of their lives. It just may be.

The Dalai Lama once said, "The more we take the welfare of others to heart and work for their benefit, the more we derive for ourselves. This is a fact we can see."

It's a great feeling to know you can make people's lives better by being of service to them, especially when ultimately you're serving yourself. Serving others activates good karma; the more you give to others, the more you will receive. By implementing and improving your service skills, you can catapult your professional career and your entire life to the next level... and reap the rewards of success.

Insight 24: Be of Service to Others

Insight 25:

Live with Humility

"To become truly great, one has to stand with people, not above them."

~ Charles de Montesquieu

O ne of the most important qualities a person aspiring to success can have is humility. Humility is defined as having a modest or humble view of one's own importance, and is widely recognized as a virtue. Humility attracts the respect of others and keeps us grounded to our values.

I have known many successful individuals and find they can be categorized into two groups: authentically successful and imitatively successful. Despite the diversity of their achievements, everyone in the authentically successful group has one thing in common and that is a humble character. The people in the imitative group, however, come across as non-original, arrogant, and boastful.

Whether you are authentically or imitatively successful is determined by the intentions behind your goals. For example, someone who promotes an inferior product for more than it is worth and then boasts about making the sale is imitatively successful. An authentically successful person would not sell such a product in the first place. Because of this commitment to honoring one's one truth, the authentically successful person will end up ahead in the long run.

David Neeleman, founder of JetBlue Airways, is a wonderful example of an authentically successful individual. Mr. Neeleman would often perform tasks that some might consider "below" his role as Jet Blue's CEO. He could often be seen cleaning the inside of a plane, working as a flight attendant, and even tagging bags. In addition, Mr. Neeleman is widely recognized for donating his entire salary to the JetBlue Crewmember Crisis Fund, established for JetBlue employees who had fallen on hard times.

Mr. Neeleman's humility not only earned him respect, but loyalty from his employees as well. When you live with humility, you will attract the best and brightest. People will want to work with you and be part of your team. When you hire the best talent, productivity is maximized. When productivity is maximized, you reap the rewards of having a profitable company. Jet Blue is a profitable company rooted in humility and enjoys a very low turnover rate.

If you would like to strive to lead a more humble life (and who wouldn't?), here are a few tips:

- **Strengthen your self-confidence.** Sometimes people with low self-confidence tend to exaggerate, or even lie, to make themselves feel important and look good in the eyes of others. This can easily be overcome by putting energy into self-development and strengthening areas of weakness. For example, a person who struggles with public speaking can study communication skills through an online resource such as www.Lynda.com or join a local Toastmasters club. Confidence is built through repetition and practice. Face your fear and it will disappear!
- **Celebrate your successes**. Don't be afraid to toot your horn when you've achieved a goal or reached a milestone. Celebrating your successes is not the same as boasting. When you celebrate a success, you come from a place of gratitude, and are fueled with well-

deserved pride. This fuel recharges your energy, whereas boasting drains your energy.

- **Celebrate the successes of others.** There's no better feeling than telling another person, "Great job! I'm proud of you!" When one person wins, we all win. Don't just recognize the accomplishments of others; offer your sincere good wishes and celebrate along with them!

- **Be teachable.** No matter how successful or smart you may be, the day you think you know it all is the day you will cease to grow. Even geniuses and experts have room to learn. Being successful in one area of life doesn't make a person an expert in everything.

- **Remember the people who helped shape your life.** There's no such thing as a self-made man or woman. Behind every great person is another person who helped them along the way. Success is always a collaborative effort. Remember and give thanks to your collaborators and share the benefits of your success.

- **Cultivate kindness.** Kindness honors and shows respect for the beauty in every person. Whatever the situation that confronts you, ask yourself, "What is the kindest way to respond?" When asked a question, respond with the truth, but offer the kindest version of the truth. Showing kindness is a valuable component for winning in life.

- **Develop understanding and compassion.** Understand that we all have different upbringings, experiences, and problems. However, we're all in this together and we all want to be loved and to feel happy.

The key ingredient for long-term success is a humble attitude. In the early years of JetBlue, David Neeleman would insist on sitting in the last row of his plane, where seats did not recline, because he felt that pleasing the customer should be more important than pleasing the CEO. By putting other people first, Mr. Neeleman built an authentically successful airline. He is proof that those who are humble will reap big rewards.

Insight 26:

Respect Yourself

"Respect your efforts, respect yourself. Self-respect leads to self-discipline. When you have both firmly under your belt, that's real power."

~Clint Eastwood

G rowing up we were all told to respect others, especially our elders and our parents and our teachers. But what we probably never heard was, "Respect yourself." Ironic, since respecting oneself is essential to the ability to respect others. Furthermore, it's essential to the ability to succeed. Without a sense of self-respect, you extinguish your potential for reaching your dreams.

Self-respect begins with honoring who you are, and being proud of who you are. Yes, life has a way of challenging us, and there may be times we feel like giving up. However, these challenges are there for a reason; they are part of the path to growth. Growth means progress, and that is what life is all about. One of my mottos is, "Each day I get better and better." When you live with self-respect, you develop the confidence and stamina to keep going and growing.

To instill and maintain self-respect, you should never allow others to make you feel bad. When you do this, you forfeit your power. I once knew someone who was so upset over the way a particular person was making her feel, her emotions started to consume every aspect of her business and personal life. Out of more than 7 billion people on this earth, that one person had all that power over her! "Wow, can I have his number?" I asked. "I have never met someone with such immense power. I would like to meet him and shake his hand."

That threw her for a loop. I then explained that anytime you give negative people attention and allow them to hurt you, in a sense you are giving them a compliment. Have enough self-respect so you keep that tremendous power for yourself! Don't allow negative people into your circle of influence. When you begin to stand up to abusive people and delete them from your life, your self-respect will rise.

Now let's go over some other steps for achieving and maintaining a high level of self-respect.

- **Celebrate your efforts and achievements**. When you see others going for their dreams, you encourage them and say, "Good job!" That is exactly how you need to feel toward yourself. Pat yourself on the back for every milestone you achieve on your path.

- **Protect yourself.** If you saw your child in harm's way, such as about to get hit by a car, certainly you would jump in to protect him or her. You must be willing to do this for yourself. No one has the right to abuse you, either verbally or physically. And when it comes to physical abuse, never extend a second chance. Period. You teach people how to treat you, and by giving someone a second chance once they abuse you, you are saying, "That's okay."

- **Set standards for yourself.** Develop the core principles for your life and write them on a paper with the heading, "My Life Principles." Allow only the people into your life who honor and respect you and your principles. This is non-negotiable.

- **Identify areas for personal improvement**. Look at these areas not as deficiencies, but as opportunities for growth. Do something every day to improve these areas.

- **Treat yourself as if you are the most important person in the world.** Believe it, because you are! Don't shortchange yourself. Accept compliments with tact and grace.

- **Maintain a positive mental attitude.** This is more than just thinking positively; it's a lifestyle. Take care of yourself physically, mentally, and spiritually. Create a positive environment by keeping a clean, clutter free home. Surround yourself with people who are productive and encouraging. In the words of Aristotle, "The antidote for fifty enemies is one friend." Never, ever allow anyone or anything to bring you down. If you join an organization, make sure you feel good about it. For example, I wouldn't want to join a religion that made me feel guilty or bad about myself.

- **Admit when you are wrong.** Make amends for any mistakes or unintentional harm you may have caused others. This shows good character. Remember, making a mistake may be only an error in judgment; repeating the same mistake over and over will put your character in question.

Self-respect is believing you are worthy of being treated well, and is at the core how you treat yourself. Invest one hour of each day to improve your life and enhance your sense of self-respect. Take 60 minutes to go to the gym or read an article or two in your area of expertise. That equals only 4 percent of your day, and you will see an amazing transformation.

So what's stopping you?

Insight 26: Respect Yourself

Insight 27:

Use the Athlete's Secret Weapon

"Bodybuilding_is much like any other sport. To be successful, you must dedicate yourself 100% to your training, diet and mental approach."

~Arnold Schwarzenegger

Since the ancient Greeks created the Olympic Games, sports have been a prominent part of cultures around the world. Today most of us think of sports primarily as an outlet for entertainment, but we can also learn so much from the techniques athletes use to win at their games.

Olympic gold medal winner Bruce Jenner said, "I always felt that my greatest asset was not my physical ability. It was my mental ability." Yes, physical conditioning is very important. However, a faulty mental attitude can ruin everything. For example, let's say two opposing tennis players are of comparable physical condition and talent. One has exceptional mental conditioning, the other has been experiencing personal turmoil. Which one would you bet on?

It's no wonder that factors such as increased stress and anxiety can negatively affect an athlete's performance. But what kind of mental state provides a winning edge? Sports psychologists have identified four ingredients for winning: Concentration, Confidence, Control and Commitment. The "4 C's" make all the difference between an average athlete and one that is superior.

So can the winning mental strategies used in sports also be used as a foundation for self-leadership and winning in life? I say, absolutely! Let's take a closer look at the 4 C's.

- **Concentration** - Concentration is the ability to focus and not allow distractions to pull you from completing the task at hand. What you pay attention to grows, and the opposite is true as well. When your focus is pulled away from your goals, they find a way to leave your life. To strengthen your concentration, train your mind to remain in the present, focusing on what it is you are trying to accomplish. Techniques for relaxation and visualization, such as yoga and meditation, can help. Think of how a golfer maintains focus on an important putt, sometimes with millions of people watching. The rest of the world can wait!

- **Confidence** - Confidence is the belief in one's own ability. Lack of belief can keep you from realizing your amazing potential. Embrace the philosophy that you are worthy, willing, and able. To boost your confidence, write a unique personal self affirmation. Believe it and repeat it often. Muhammad Ali's affirmation was, "I am the greatest." This quote by Napoleon Hill, author of the classic book *Think and Grow Rich*, sums it perfectly: "Whatever you conceive and believe, you will achieve."

- **Control** - Control is the ability to maintain emotional serenity regardless of the situation. The best way to remain in control is to accept responsibility for the things that are within your realm of control and to let go of those that aren't. Think of your mind as a business control center in charge of your life and you are the manager. If you don't take control of your thinking, then society and the media will do it for you. Forfeiting your control is nothing more than willfully accepting mental slavery.

- **Commitment** - Commitment is a vow to make a determined effort to pursue a goal until it is reached. Maintaining your commitment is easier when you have a support system in place, so be sure to surround yourself with positive people. Recognize the value of each step you take toward your goal and take at least one step every day. Visualize yourself achieving your goal, and always remember the purpose behind your actions.

Your life is not a game, but by integrating the concepts used by the greatest athletes on earth, you can live better than you could ever imagine. Utilizing and practicing this model can have a positive effect in your personal, social and business lives. Study the 4 C's and identify the areas where there's room for improvement. Apply the 4 C's to those areas. Give them your full attention. Let the 4 C's be your guidelines for living each day and claim what it is you want to achieve!

Insight 27: Use the Athlete's Secret Weapon

Insight 28:

Personalize the Pareto Principle

"Surround yourself with the best people you can find."

~Ronald Reagan

According to the Pareto principle, created by an Italian economist named Vilfredo Pareto, 20 percent of the population controls 80 percent of the wealth. Also known as The 80-20 Rule and The Law of the Vital Few, this principle has a variety of applications. It means that in any set of things, 20 percent are vital and 80 percent are trivial.

I don't believe anyone starting a new career or opening a new business sets out to be in the bottom percentile of success. But how can you secure your place in the top 20 percent? What qualities give an individual or a business that "elite factor"?

One way to differentiate yourself or your business is by connecting with others. Here are some strategies for building relationships so strong that no one can compete with you.

- **Create a personal customer experience.** Cheryl Sommer is the owner of Kaune's Neighborhood Market, a small independent grocery store. In a business dominated by giants, Ms. Sommer identified where her competitors were lacking, which also happened to be her company's strength: personalization. Customers walking into a Kaune's Neighbor-hood Market, are greeted like friends. Employees offer genuine smiles, sometimes call customers by their first names, and even give an occasional hug. People look forward to the shopping experience Kaune's provides. Ms. Sommer increased her odds of success by targeting the top 20 percent of the characteristics that resulted in success. She focused on her mission and hired great people to take care of her great customers. By creating a personal customer experience, she brought the neighborhood concept that everyone loves to life.

- **Make your customers feel like a million bucks.** Always treat people with excellence. Imagine how great a feeling it would be to hear people say things like, "No one has ever done anything like this for me before." Even if you have a competitor offering the exact service, when you build friendships you will retain clients for life. Anytime a client or prospect finishes an encounter with you or your establishment, they should feel better than when they arrived. I personally have driven extra miles to do business with a company just because of how they made me feel, even though I could have found the same product much closer to my house. They knew my name, smiled, and asked about me. Consumers are more loyal to people than they are to products. People may forget many things; however, they will never forget how you made them feel. And never underestimate the value of a smile.

- **Be consistent**. People should expect and receive the same quality service each and every time, regardless of whether it's almost closing time or if you or a staff member is feeling down due to personal problems.

Never let what's going on outside of the workplace transcend into the customers' space. If employees bring drama into the workplace, stop it quickly or send them home. Consistently meeting customer expectations will result in customer loyalty, so never deviate and stay consistent. The second you lose consistency, you will begin to lose business.

- **Eliminate distractions.** Your full attention is one of the greatest gifts you can give to a person. Calls on your cell phone can wait. When talking with or servicing customers, make them feel there is nothing else on earth that you'd rather be doing. Listen intently to what they are saying.

- **"Mission First, People Always."** This motto has been used by the U.S. military. It acknowledges that the mission is the main objective and is very important; however, in order to complete the mission, you need great people.

So, you want to leverage your time and focus on the 20 percent that really matters, the areas that produce the most results and have the most impact. Typically, this will come down to how you treat others. A professional boxer sleeps, eats and breathes boxing when training for a fight, nothing else. You must practice this same diligence.

Regardless of whom your competition may be, you can increase your chances dramatically and join the elite with these simple yet powerful strategies.

Insight 28: Personalize the Pareto Principle

Insight 29:

Project Self-Confidence

"Every small positive change we make in ourselves repays us in confidence in the future."

~Alice Walker

I t's easy to understand why we procrastinate on undesirable tasks. But often we hold back from doing things we actually *want* to do--something like asking a person for a date or asking for a raise or an opportunity to speak to an audience. What is at the root of such resistance? The answer is the fear of failure.

Inhibitions, doubt, fear, and anxiety can halt our desires and our aspirations of what we want to do, become, or have in life. Fortunately, these can be overcome. By increasing our self-confidence, we can conquer these barriers and live a powerful life with no regrets.

Self-confidence is all about having a strong belief in yourself and your abilities. Your level of self-confidence is rooted in how you feel on the inside; it has nothing to do with being skinny, fat, tall, short, rich or poor. You can be any combination of these and still be self-confident.

Although self-confidence is not dependant on your outside circumstances, it can certainly improve them. The key is to build your confidence so high that no matter what, you are

121

comfortable with yourself the way you are. And *then* if you'd like to get skinnier or wealthier, you have confidence to help you achieve it.

I believe that everyone can benefit tremendously from improving their self-confidence, and if you agree with me, then read on. Here are some of my favorite tips:

- **Put your own needs first.** Many people have a habit of placing others' needs above their own. Although this may seem like a noble act, I call it dodging personal responsibility. You owe it to yourself to consider your own needs first, just as you're advised when flying to secure your own oxygen mask before attending to someone else. Remember, by putting yourself first and becoming the best you can be, you can be of better service to others.

- **Know what you want.** Would you ever go into a car dealership and simply say, "I'd like to buy a car?" Although any salesman would be more than happy to help you, you've essentially given away your control over the situation and your sense of power. This lack of knowledge and associated self-confidence can be very costly. Do you think you might get a better deal if you do your research beforehand and know exactly what vehicle you want?

- **Find the holes in your excuses.** For example, let's say you dream of becoming a successful real estate agent. However, your self-talk goes something like, "I don't have much time," or "I'm a single parent and barely can make ends meet." How many people would you say in this entire world have been in similar situations and went on to become successful real estate agents? One? Ten? More than a hundred? Yes, of course. If others in the same circumstances could achieve your goal, so can you.

- **Practice active listening and respond authentically.** Self-confident individuals are great communicators. A great communicator speaks with specificity and clarity, but most importantly they listen intently and wait before responding. They speak with genuine concern and show respect by not rushing or checking the time. To help improve your speaking skills, consider joining a speaker's group or Toastmasters International.

- **Surround yourself with people who believe in you.** Identify the individuals who think the world of you and who lift you up when you're feeling down. I refer to them as your personal cheering team. Make it a point to schedule some time with these team members—why wait for a low period to hit?

- **Look and feel your best.** The better we look and feel, the more confident we become. It's important to stay fit, eat healthy foods, and keep yourself looking stylish. There's a saying, "If you see a woman and she's dressed sloppily, you notice how she's dressed. If you see a woman and she's dressed impeccably, you notice the woman." Of course, the same goes for men. Make sure you're noticed for the right reason!

- **Face the fear and it will disappear.** Chances are you've done this before. Think about things that once scared you. Perhaps it was riding a bike or swimming in the deep end of a pool. That fear may now seem funny to you, but in retrospect, how did you overcome your fear? Can you use the same strategies to address the fears that are holding you back now?

- **Release the negative events of the past.** This is essential in order to move forward. Perhaps you were laughed at or bullied as a child, or endured some other trauma. By releasing the negativity, we stop the pattern of re-victimizing ourselves over and over again.

- **Learn to relax.** It is essential to take a break from life's events. This is very important because your mind needs to be in a relaxed state in order to organize your thoughts and reflect on your goals. Choose your preferred mode of relaxation, whether it's meditation, massage, yoga, or simply listening to some relaxing music with the lights off.

- **Believe in your worthiness.** Who is the most important person in the world? You are, so act like it! Become the center of your own universe. That's what you really are!

All of these strategies will strengthen your self-confidence. As you develop self-confidence, you accept accountability for your life and become resilient when problems arise. You give yourself the freedom to express who you truly are, without worrying how others may judge you. And most importantly, you can overcome the fear of failure and find yourself on the road to achieving your goals.

Insight 30:

Complete What You Start

"Good business leaders create a vision, articulate the vision, passionately own the vision, and relentlessly drive it to completion."

~ Jack Welch

T he difference between a life truly fulfilled and one that is not can be a matter of simply completing the goals we set out for ourselves, both big and small.

In today's cluttered world most of us seem to have a "too busy," "not enough time," or "put things off for another day" attitude. But imagine if everyone actually finished what they started. How packed would a health club be if everyone who joined actually went? How empty would the doctor's office be if everyone kept up with the health regimen of their New Year's resolutions? How many volumes of books and works of art would be created to inspire others?

Think of all the projects you've begun and never completed, even if some of those projects got only as far as a thought in that direction. Is there a book you wanted to write or a business you intended to start? A diet or exercise plan you began in earnest but never completed? Perhaps there's a black belt you've always aspired to or college a course you've always been meaning to take.

Whatever it may be, the sense of incompletion saps your energy and can have a lasting negative effect in your life. When you leave certain goals incomplete, you a feel a sense of loss for what could have been. This creates negative energy and emotions. Now take a moment and consider what your life would be like if you had completed all those projects you began. How would you feel? Empowered, no doubt.

We have those feelings for a reason. Think of it this way: If you cut your finger, you'd give it attention, right? You'd nurse it, put a Band-Aid on it, and it would heal. The same concept applies to that sense of incompletion; it's your minds way of saying you have something that needs attention. The cure is to give it your undivided attention.

Let's revisit those abandoned projects. Make a list of everything you began and never completed. Include items that may have been merely a twinkle in your eye. Maybe they never came to fruition because you were going through difficult times or you got distracted by others who told you your goal was not worthy or possible.

Now review your list and cross out anything that is no longer relevant or of importance. Your list at this point consists of the things you are going to complete, not what you'd like to complete. The key now is to be very clear about your goals. Visualize the feeling of completing each task. Begin with the simplest one. When you complete your first task, keep that energy and momentum going. Move on to the next one. Focus on one thing at a time. They say the way to kill a man with a dream is to give him several, so complete one goal before moving on to the next.

Here are some tips to help you reach the joy of completeness:

- **Start your day by planning your day.** Within the first hour of waking up, organize your thoughts so you can focus on the things that matter and have lasting value in your life. Write down your goals for the day and structure your time around them. Stay on course and keep the values of your goals in mind.

- **Maintain a pursuit of excellence.** Keep yourself motivated, focused and knowledgeable. Constantly feed your mind positive and creative knowledge with books, audio programs and mentors.
- **Eliminate distractions.** To achieve your goals, you must be able to concentrate and focus, and your ability to concentrate and focus is directly proportional to your ability to eliminate distraction. Distraction creates obstacles that pull you away from completing your goals; it is the killer of dreams. This is where effective self-management comes in.
- **Assemble a team of supporters.** Your team should include people with similar goals who will support each other, instill accountability, and make sure everyone stays on course.
- **Do a daily audit**. At the end of the day, assess how much time you dedicated to your important goals. Did you complete what you set out to do?

If you never complete what you begin, you will never know the joy that completion will bring. Become a finisher in your own life, and develop a stellar reputation as the one that gets things done. Give yourself the gift of completion so that you can remove any negative emotional residue you may be feeling, and move forward with your life.

Insight 30: Complete What You Start

Insight 31:

Practice Positive Intrinsic Motivation

"You can't build a reputation on what you are going to do."

~Henry Ford

A sense of achievement is a vital force required for a joyful and fulfilled life, and learning to maintain your motivation toward your desired goals is crucial. Many people consider me to be a motivator, but would it surprise you if I told you I can't motivate anyone? That's because everyone is already 100 percent motivated 100 percent of the time. The catch is, they are motivated either positively or negatively. Someone may be negatively motivated to lie on the couch and do nothing, or positively motivated to build their own business. All I can do is help people become aware of what they truly want out of life, and help redirect their thinking toward the positive.

One of the biggest traps you can fall into is the feeling of de-motivation toward goals that would bring you joy and fulfillment. The key to combating de-motivation, and achieving success is to maintain a state of *positive intrinsic motivation.* This type of motivation comes from within, from your heart. It's fueled by three components--energy, passion, and enthusiasm--and a deep, burning desire that propels you into action. For example, if you were an aspiring opera singer dreaming of performing in an ornate opera house in front of thousands of people, you would passionately and enthusiastically exert energy for countless hours to achieve that goal.

Everyone has their own individual goals, whether it's to walk one block or to climb Mount Everest. What's important is not the size of the goal, but the value of the achievement to the individual. Positive intrinsic motivation is at the root of all of the greatest achievements in the world, including those by the Wright brothers, who invented the first successful airplane, and Roger Bannister, the first man to break the four-minute mile. (And by the way, both of those goals were once thought to be unreachable.)

Here are some strategies to help you tap into the immense power of positive intrinsic motivation:

- **Wake up!** By this I mean, increase your level of awareness. What excites you more than anything? What do you dream about becoming, doing, or having? In other words, what is your burning desire? Remember, you cannot create something without an initial thought, and you cannot change something if you don't know it exists.

- **Delete negativity.** Considering how we're constantly bombarded with stories of violence and sadness in the evening news or with friends and co-workers lamenting over the drama in their lives, it's easy to see how our thinking can get clouded with negativity. To combat this, we must take time to vacuum out the negative residue. How? By limiting our exposure to the media, holding only positive conversations, reading motivational books, listening to inspiring music, and by scheduling some solitary, quiet time to reconnect with our inner selves.

- **Visualize yourself achieving your goals.** Visualize *in detail* exactly how you would feel the moment when you achieve your goals. Bask in that feeling, and hold on to it. For example, if you're going through the challenges of medical school, you could visualize how you would feel the day you receive your diploma, surrounded by your family and friends smiling with pride. This will motivate you to focus your energy on attaining your goal.

- **Create a physical representation of your achievement.** Let's say your goal is to lose weight. Photoshop an image of yourself depicting what you will look like at your ideal weight. Post that photo on your refrigerator and use it as a screensaver on your cell phone and computer. This will serve as a reminder to stay on course.

- **Monitor your self-talk.** What do you continually tell yourself? Take a moment right now, and think of what you told yourself upon waking up this morning, or 10 minutes ago. Was it positive or negative? Are you talking about what's going right in your life, or what's not? Are you focusing on problems or solutions? Everything you tell yourself is an affirmation, so make sure your self-talk sounds like a master motivator is speaking to you.

- **Remember, it's all up to you.** This is your life and your goals, no one else's. Be willing to stand alone if necessary, and depend on no one. What others may think should have no relevance to your burning desire and what's important to you. You do not need the approval of others.

When we stay on course following our life's goals, we become more powerful people. Always remember your unique journey and why you must do it. Strengthening and mastering the skills of powerful intrinsic motivation will help keep your heart strong and your doubts weak.

131

Now get to work!

Insight 32:

Follow the Law of Qualification

"In action a great heart is the chief qualification. In work, a great head."

~ Arthur Schopenhauer

E verything in life is a qualification. Since the day we are born, life is nothing more than a series of qualifying events. To enter kindergarten, we must qualify. To graduate from college, we must qualify. To get a job, we must qualify. To get a mortgage, we must qualify. You get the picture.

The Law of Qualification is a concept I developed; however, its principles have been used by world leaders for centuries. Its tenet is, "In order to achieve any goal, there is a process, and only through that process one qualifies to achieve that goal." It is about personal responsibility and self-leadership, and if you follow the correct process without deviating from it, you will achieve your desired results.

Everything has a process, just like growing a garden. First you need the proper nourishing soil, and then you plant and water the seeds. In due time you will reap a beautiful garden.

If you bypass any of these steps, you will end up with no garden at all or a very poor one.

But what is the correct process? That's simple—all we have to do is follow the instructions. And the good news is, the Internet is full of information detailing the step-by-step, tried and proven ways of how other individuals have already done it. They have made it easier for us! Going through the process, you will have moments of discovery and new understanding.

My friend Darren LaCroix, who earned first place out of 25,000 contestants in the World Championship of Public Speaking, says it best: "If you shortcut the process, you shortcut the results." Trust me, at one point of his life, Darren could have been named the world's worst public speaker. Yet he went on to become one of the best. Why? Because he understood The Law of Qualification.

He knew there was a process he had to follow in order to qualify to become the best. Darren sought advice from others who had already accomplished similar goals, and he got a coach—an expert at what he wanted to achieve. He did what the coach told him to do, and wasn't afraid to fail and keep going until he got it right. Darren practiced, practiced, and practiced some more. He never turned down an opportunity to speak, and now his motto is, "Stage time, stage time, stage time."

Anything worthwhile in life must be earned. We must be willing to put in the necessary work to reap the rewards. Think about how impressed you'd be upon meeting a brain surgeon, a top athlete, or a world famous innovator. What you are really impressed by is the time, energy, and dedication required to qualify to become who they've become and accomplish what they have. These types of individuals did not skip steps or cheat, and did not deviate from their goals. No, they stuck with it.

Now let's go over some principles for applying the Law of Qualification.

- **Stay on course and never deviate from the process**. The second you move away from the process, you begin to head away from your goal.
- **Don't try to bypass the process**. Be willing to put in the work. Many people complain about what they don't have, but aren't willing to do what it takes to achieve what they want. For example, they might want an amazingly fit body, but don't want to watch their diet or spend time in the gym. They would rather take a drug or endure surgery. In other words, it's easier to bypass the process. But that's not the path to achievement.
- **Invest in yourself on a daily basis**. Do something every day to bring yourself closer to your goals. Exercise, study... know what the process is and take the required steps.
- **Listen to expert advice**. Search out those who have already done it and ask them to share their experience.
- **Do as a puppy does: be authentically enthusiastic**! With enthusiasm your success rate increases phenomenally and you may even attract other people wanting to help you qualify.
- **Maintain your focus on the joy of attaining the goal, not how hard it is to get there**. Always keep your goal in the forefront of your mind, with persistence and passion.

Darren LaCroix utilized the Law of Qualification and went from being the worst to finishing in first place. Imagine what you can do if you simply follow the directions that are already written and waiting for you to apply them. All great accomplishments began by following a process—how do you think the astronauts landed on the moon? So whether you want to write a book, be a successful business owner, a teacher, or a doctor... remember that getting there is a process, and through that process you must qualify. It may not be easy, but it sure will be worth it!

Now figure out what it is that you want, find out what you must do to qualify, commit to action and *go for it*.

Insight 33:

Discover the Authentic "You"

"I had no idea that being your authentic self could make me as rich as I've become. If I had, I'd have done it a lot earlier."

~ Oprah Winfrey

I t goes without saying that we come into this life being totally dependent—we depend on our parents to feed us, protect us and educate us. But in the process we learn to become independent, much like a bird when it leaves its mothers nest. From that point on, it depends on itself in its journey through life.

Humans, however, tend to remain dependent on others after they've "left the nest," even when it comes to their success and happiness. And somewhere along the way, we lose our sense of purpose, our true identity. We lose sight of who we are and what we are supposed to do.

We see this dependency play itself out over and over. Why do people hold debt? Because they became dependent on credit cards. Why do they become sad after a romantic breakup? Because they became dependent on someone else for their happiness. Why are many people unhappy with their jobs? Because they are in a position that is not suited to their true self. Why do many people stay in an unhappy relationship? Because they are not with the best person for them, and are too lazy or fearful to make a change.

The science of living as fully as possible begins with living your authentic self. When you do this, you automatically begin to align yourself with what has the most meaning to you. This includes your ideal vocation, relationships and finances. Sometimes living authentically is just a matter of letting go of what you *don't* want so you can make room for what you *do* want. In reality the only reason we may have negative people and situations in our lives is because we hold on to them, so LET GO!

When you rely on others, you transfer your power away from you. Do you have feelings of frustration, fear, emptiness or incompleteness? You may have a very lucrative life and still have these feelings because you are not expressing your true self. When you're not living authentically, all you are doing is surviving. When you stand up to negative forces in your life, it's because the true authentic you is beginning to emerge. And it's your right to stand up for yourself, your beliefs, and your individuality—so stand up, stand out and embrace your unique authentic self!

I admit it can be easier to just go along with the expectations of others and put our own aspirations on the back burner. All this does is diminish your power. It imprisons the purpose of who you truly are and what you are meant to do with your life. Do not succumb to this type of thinking. Listen to your own needs, wants, and intuition. Your fears, worries, and overall stress levels are magnified when you are not aligned with your authentic self.

When you meet someone who is being their authentic self, you sense their conviction, their fearless passion for life. And deep inside you know that's where you want to be. That's why we are here--to create a better life and do things right. So here are some tips for aligning your actions with the authentic "you":

- **Start where your energy is.** Write down the elements that stimulate you intrinsically. What do you care about? What makes you mad? When Abraham Lincoln witnessed slaves being sold away from their families, he clenched his fist in anger and vowed that one day he would do something to stop slavery. He cared so deeply and channeled his anger productively, and as president of the United States, he abolished slavery.

- **Do what you love**. Steve Jobs said that the only thing that kept him going through all the tough times was that he loved what he did. Imagine creating a life on the basis of what you love, actually doing it, and having a blast doing it!

- **Make the time**. Someone who says they are too busy to pursue their ideal life simply does not have their priorities in order. We must make time for what really matters.

- **Believe in your power**. Worry comes in the belief that you are powerless. Write down who you are, not what you do. Claim the power that is you!

- **Take ownership of who you are**. Have faith in your own voice. Think for yourself, develop and share your unique ideas.

- **Look at those who are living the life you desire with inspiration, not envy**. How can you learn from them? What are they doing that you should be integrating into your own life?

- **Think of how you would express yourself if you removed some of your current limiting beliefs.** What would your life be like? Remember, some things you once believed as a child, you now believe as untrue. Preconceived beliefs and notions hinder growth of knowledge.

- **Avoid conformity.** The need to fit in with others can rob you of living your authentic life. Stop worrying about what others may think or say. All this does is hold you back, and if you listen long enough you will end up believing them.

Remember, if we don't go within, we end up going without. We are living in time where trusting and depending on others is like a game of Russian roulette. For this reason we must have full faith, trust, and conviction in ourselves... our authentic selves. Take a stand and trust in your own capabilities talents and abilities and be prepared to be amazed. A whole new world will appear before your very eyes.

Insight 34:

Make Decisions Consciously

"Whenever you see a successful business, someone once made a courageous decision."

~Peter Drucker

T his insight is best illustrated by the following case study.

Stormy Simon is a divorced mother of two. After her marriage ended she made ends meet with the support of welfare. While she doesn't have a college education, she learned early on that she needed to be successful in order to provide for her sons.

So how did she become the top executive of a $1.5 billion company? I had the opportunity to ask her.

Her response: *"I made a conscious decision of where I was going to put my energy."*

Stormy did some soul searching to figure out what she wanted to do. She came across an innovative new company called Overstock.com and after doing some research, Stormy concluded it would be the company she'd focus her energy on.

She applied for a position and was hired as a temporary sales agent.

At the time, Overstock.com was just two years old and Stormy was about its sixty-fifth employee. While the company was still relatively small, she had the opportunity to work closely with the CEO, Patrick M. Byrne. Whenever Mr. Byrne had a task to be done or needed help with a problem, he would ask, "Who wants in?" Stormy would be the first to shoot her hand up enthusiastically and respond, "I'm in!" She was not afraid to offer help where it was needed. "I saw where there was a huge amount to be done, and I was happy to do it," she told me.

It wouldn't be long until Stormy was recognized as a valuable asset and a dedicated employee who deserved to be promoted. She rose from sales agent to Director of Business-to-Business, and in 2003 she created the Books, Music and Movies department, a division she spearheaded from its inception.

Stormy Simon then took over Overstock's Customer Care functions. She worked diligently to restructure the department by setting up cross-functional teams, creating educational programs for agents, and implementing customer relationship management (CRM) software to improve response times. Under her direction the company gained traction for its superior customer service, and since 2007 Overstock has consistently ranked in the Top 5 in customer service by the National Retail Federation/ American Express Customer Service Survey.

In 2009, Stormy was named chief marketing officer, appointed to oversee the direction of the company's marketing and advertising department. She wrote and produced Overstock's iconic television ads, which she often appeared in. She continued to climb the career ladder, and became the senior vice president of customer and partner care. In 2013, she earned the title of co-president and in 2014 Stormy was named president.

As would anyone holding such a position, Stormy puts long hours. However, she does not consider herself to be a workaholic; she manages her time strategically. Demonstrating her appreciation for work-life balance, she takes time off for vacations and encourages others to do the same. Her philosophy is, "When you begin to feel grumpy, take time off. There's always tomorrow. There's always another 60 hours next week if all doesn't get done, so there's no need to stress."

A typical day for Stormy is meetings, meetings and more meetings and answering thousands of emails personally. She enjoys going to work each and every day. "Each day feels like a brand new day," she says. Stormy believes it's important to feel happy and excited about your job, and that working should be fun. "Work to live, not live to work," is her motto.

Employee input is key at Overstock.com. All employees (currently numbering approximately 1600) are encouraged to submit their ideas, which are read and reviewed by their peers, without fear of retribution. "Our goal is to work in collaboration, as opposed to working alone," Stormy says, citing that the contributions of many minds is essential for the company's evolution. "We don't all have to agree, but we do have to respect everyone's message."

The intention is for all employees to feel empowered and happy, and to feel like they're part of a family. And having fun is an essential ingredient; the company even had rapper Snoop Dog perform at a corporate event.

Stormy Simon became the CEO of her own life and in the process, held an instrumental role in developing the Overstock.com brand into a worldwide online giant. She saw the opportunity, the company's potential, and made a conscious decision to commit her energy fully with enthusiasm.

Stormy didn't allow anything or anyone to distract her—no "Scattered Thinking Syndrome" there—and made herself available to embrace and help solve any problems that needed to be addressed. In retrospect, she admits, "There were many times I put the company first. The opportunity was so great that I had to make tough decisions on how to spend my time. Being older and wiser, I'm not sure I would make the same decisions as the company is still here, and my boys have grown."

Nonetheless, Stormy has been a great service to others, with a commitment to living with integrity. Most of all, she repositioned and empowered herself, and went on to succeed in bad times.

From a temporary worker to president of a $1.5 billion online retailer, Stormy Simon's meteoric rise demonstrates the power of making decisions consciously.

Insight 35:

Be Happy Now

"Happiness is the meaning and the purpose of life, the whole aim and end of human existence."

~Aristotle

I magine yourself as a superhero with a superpower that could convert stress, fear, and worry into love, gratitude, and understanding. This would be the ultimate superpower because you would be living in a state of happiness.

So many people go through life on a constant journey, searching for happiness like it's some kind of futuristic goal. They say things like, "When I get a new job, then I will be happy" and "I'll be happy when I pay off my home" or "when I find a mate" or "when I graduate from school." And then there's my favorite: "I'll be happy once I lose 30 pounds." The list is endless.

Happiness is a state of being, not a destination. Making your happiness dependent upon another individual or future event or possession is nothing more than self-imposed suffering. This type of thinking not only keeps us from experiencing happiness, but also our most powerful and important position in life: the present moment!

The present moment is so important because it's the only time we can exercise our full power and experience happiness. We can do things only in the now, and all we ever have is the now. If you find this hard to believe, do something yesterday. Tomorrow is not here yet, and when it does get here, it will become now.

To help you better understand this concept, ask yourself, "When do I feel stress or worry?" You will find that your answer will be relative to an event in the past or something that you fear will happen in the future. Anytime you deny the present moment you open a portal for attracting stress, fear and worry. If you catch your mind wandering in the past, think about amazing and happy times, and if you wander into the future, visualize your best possible outcome.

When we are happy, we have everything. By making our happiness our #1 priority, we can begin to attract everything we need for living and sustaining a joyful and powerful life.

And guess what? You already possess the happiness superpower. All you have to do is to reconnect with the happiness that lies within and practice happiness strategies until they become habit. Here are some ideas to help you uncover your amazing superpower:

- **Look on the bright side.** The way in which we interpret the world around us is key. Believe that there is a positive force behind every occurrence, no matter how bad it may seem.
- **Live with a sense of purpose.** What would you dare to become if you knew you could not fail? If you could be known for one great accomplishment on this earth, what would it be? The answers will help reveal your true life's purpose.
- **Seize the opportunity to serve others.** Notice the sense of fulfillment you feel when you help someone, fix something, or make something better.

- **Release what does not serve you.** Scrub your brain of thoughts that only bring you down. Clean out your closet or garage and let go of whatever is not working in your life.

- **Flip that thought.** The next time you catch yourself with a negative thought, challenge yourself to flip it around and replace it with a contrasting positive thought. For example, instead of saying, "I hate watching violent television programs," flip the thought to, "I enjoy watching positive and uplifting shows.

- **Choose joyful acceptance over grief.** Of course we grieve when we lose someone dear. However, carrying sadness can prolong suffering. For example, instead of being sad when looking at a photo of someone you've lost, be grateful for having had that person in your life. Honor their memory, and share those happy memories with others.

- **Always strive for excellence.** Doing everything to your very best ability results in a sense of pride and instills confidence, which translates to happiness in your life.

- **Balance the physical, mental, and spiritual.** Personally, when I start each day I envision three empty cups: one for the physical, the mental and the spiritual aspects of life. I then try to fill each cup as evenly as possible. As I reflect on the day, I know which area I have to work on more.

- **Adopt an attitude of gratitude.** Here's an exercise I developed which is a real eye opener. Make a list of five things you are grateful for such as your family, your eyesight, your health. Choose one of those items and picture what your life would be like without it. Then take away another item on the list. Now what would your life be like? And then take away another. Nothing will cultivate a deeper appreciation for what you have than the thought of living without it.

Choose to uncover your happiness superpower! Life will never be perfect; adversities and problems will follow us until we leave this earth. But anytime you start to feel down, you can always unleash your superpower with three simple words: "Be happy now."

About the Author

Nikkos (Nikk) Zorbas is a leader in self-development who has inspired millions through his bestselling books Discovering Your Personal Power and The Reveal, as well as his music, monthly columns and educational workshops. Using the science of extraordinary achievement, Mr. Zorbas can teach you how to discover your personal power and pave the path to success.

For details about speeches, seminars and coaching, please visit: www.NikkosZorbas.com

For inspirational music, please visit: www.LawofAttractionMusic.com

Nikkos would love to hear about your personal experience with his work. Please share your thoughts with him at Nikk@NikkZorbas.com

If you haven't already - check out Nikk's #1 bestseller:

Discovering Your Personal Power: 27 Articles of Inspiration

NOTES

NOTES

NOTES

www.ingramcontent.com/pod-product-compliance
Lightning Source LLC
Chambersburg PA
CBHW051706170526
45167CB00002B/559